THE
CAMPING
LIFE

THE
CAMPING
LIFE

INSPIRATION AND IDEAS
FOR ENDLESS ADVENTURES

BRENDAN LEONARD | FOREST WOODWARD

ARTISAN | NEW YORK

"SOMETIMES ALL YOU NEED IS TO
CLIMB A SIMPLE HILL, TO SPEND TIME
STARING AT AN EMPTY HORIZON,
TO JUMP INTO A COLD RIVER OR SLEEP
UNDER THE STARS, OR PERHAPS SHARE
A WHISKY AT A SMALL COUNTRY INN
IN ORDER TO REMIND YOURSELF WHAT
MATTERS MOST TO YOU IN LIFE."

—ALASTAIR HUMPHREYS,
*MICROADVENTURES: LOCAL DISCOVERIES
FOR GREAT ESCAPES*

Contents

Introduction
by Brendan Leonard

While scrolling through my phone one day, I came across an interesting quote about nature: how a huge number of us were discovering we needed it as an antidote to our hyperconnected, always-on, drinking-from-the-data-firehose lives. It was a pertinent quote for 2020, when you might find yourself in a coffee shop, looking up from your laptop to take a five-second break from fifteen open browser tabs and ever-multiplying e-mails and see everyone else looking at some sort of glowing screen or two, trying to keep up with their own personalized stream of information.

Except the quote I read was not from 2020—it was from 1901, when John Muir wrote it in *Our National Parks*:

> Thousands of tired, nerve-shaken, over-civilized people are beginning to find out that going to the mountains is going home; that wildness is a necessity.

If John Muir noticed in 1901 that people needed wildness to deal with "civilization"—back before e-mail, before texting, before cell phones—imagine what he would think now. And how much more we probably need wildness in our lives these days, with our overflowing inboxes, pocket computers that buzz with notifications all day, and twenty-four-hour news cycles.

There's a real thing that happens to all of us when we run away from all that electronic chatter and into the wildness John Muir was talking about: As we drive away from cities and towns and toward the mountains or forests, we notice that our cell service is gradually becoming spotty. We become anxious at first: *What if someone at work needs to get a hold of me?* (Yes, even on Saturday.) *What if I miss something on Instagram or Twitter? What if some sort of national news happens and I don't read an article about it right away, or for a day or two?* We rapid-fire through apps, trying to get one last update before we lose contact.

As we drive farther, our cell phone service fades more and more. Eventually, we arrive at a campground or at a trailhead where we begin walking or biking to a campsite somewhere. At some point, we either lose cell service altogether or we become frustrated trying to refresh our e-mail inbox with one lone bar of service, and we give up. Our phones are now useless. We have no choice: We are present. In nature.

Somehow, without a constant stream of data, we manage to fill the time: setting up tents, unrolling sleeping bags, sitting on rocks, maybe reading paperbacks, walking to waterfalls or mountain views, building campfires and sitting and staring at them as if they were streaming consecutive episodes of our favorite Netflix shows. And we're fine.

The more days we're away from the information-industrial complex and in the woods, the less we care. Sure, maybe we miss our spouse, friends, parents, or kids, but not so much our office, and definitely not social media or the news—the only news we need is whether it's going to rain today. After a couple of days, we may wonder if we actually need to go back to our house, our to-do lists, our job at all. Certainly if anything has come up at work after two or three days, everyone at the office has figured out the solution by now, right? Can't we just live here, with no e-mail and with campfires every night?

Of course, we can't, and we all eventually go back to civilization. But on returning, we have memories, some stories, and photos we might put on our end-of-year holiday cards. By getting away from all the stuff we think we need on a daily (or hourly) basis, we've created something memorable, a narrative that rises above all the information wrangling and logistics of our everyday lives. We have something to talk about when someone asks, "What have you been up to?"

John Muir famously would take off into the Sierra Nevada range with hardly any supplies or equipment besides a bit of bread and tea, and he once spent the night near the snow-covered summit of Mount Shasta in California, next to a volcanic steam vent for warmth. Thankfully, we have much improved equipment and food nowadays, and "roughing it" can be a lot less rough.

This book is designed to inspire you to step away from the noise and get out there, whether "out there" is one-night camping at a state or county park thirty minutes from your house, a weeklong hut-to-hut trip in the Alps, or a sixteen-day raft trip through the Grand Canyon. We're all busy, and any time away is a gift, even if it's a weekend or two a year.

To immerse yourself in the outdoor experience, you don't have to sleep on a portalege suspended a thousand feet up a rock-climbing route or in a tent on a snowfield at ten thousand feet on the side of a volcano (although we'll

cover these styles of camping). The point of a night in a campground with flush toilets and a night out in the desert twenty miles from the nearest road is the same: Connecting with nature. Feeling the wind on your face, listening to raindrops on a tent fly, breathing air filtered by a stand of pine trees. And not caring if you have mud on your shoes or if your clothes smell like campfire smoke.

One of the most famous Muir quotes—you've surely seen it on a T-shirt, sticker, or Instagram bio—is "The mountains are calling and I must go." For sure, we're in a moment on this planet where we all have a million things pulling at us—but we can still hear that call from the mountains. Or the desert or the forest or the river. And it's arguably one of the most important— or at least one of the most memorable—calls we can answer.

Packing List:
All-Purpose Camping Gear

Tent

You don't need to spend several hundred dollars on a tent, but, of course, pricey tents offer more features. Lower-priced tents are fine for car camping, but be forewarned that their corresponding rainflies are often sold separately. Confirm that your tent comes with a rainfly before you leave the store (or purchase the tent online) rather than when you get to your campsite and see rain clouds forming. Backpacking tents are more compact and lighter weight and thus more expensive. You can use a backpacking tent for car camping, but a car camping–style tent isn't great for backpacking because it's several pounds heavier and much bulkier—some can eat up all the space inside a backpack. So if you want to leave your options open, buy a backpacking tent.

Sleeping Bag

In the same vein, a backpacking (or mummy-style) sleeping bag works great for all types of camping, whereas a rectangular sleeping bag, while usually less expensive, is better suited for car camping. Rectangular bags don't pack down very small and tend to be heavier. You can purchase a decent synthetic or down mummy bag without breaking the bank, and it should last for years.

Sleeping Pad

Whether the pad is three inches thick and as comfortable as your bed at home or a half-inch-thick piece of foam, the only general rule about a sleeping pad is that your camping life will be better with one than without one. You don't need to spend a lot, and you can go as big and bulky as you want (especially if you're not squeezing the pad into a backpack). But be aware that a big, six-inch-thick air mattress holds a lot of air underneath you as you sleep, and that air can get cold in the middle of the night, making it impossible for you to stay warm and fall asleep. So bigger isn't always better. I recommend a Therm-a-Rest ProLite pad as a good basic sleeping pad or a Big Agnes Insulated Air Core Ultra for a little more cushioning.

Stove

On one end of the spectrum is the classic green Coleman two-burner propane stove. It's the size of a briefcase, available at almost any discount retail store in the United States for less than fifty dollars, and has gotten the job done for thousands of campers for decades. On the other end of the spectrum is a lightweight backpacking stove that weighs less than a pound, will work at an elevation of fifteen thousand feet, and runs on almost any type of gas. Both stoves are great for different reasons, but they both essentially do the same

thing: warm up pots that you cook your food in. If you're not planning on backpacking, a two-burner stove can handle your needs. Even the inexpensive ones work well, and you can find fuel canisters in almost any town. If you're planning on backcountry camping as well as car camping, a single-burner backpacking stove will work fine, too. It won't offer you a second burner, but generally that's a hardship only for a gourmet camp chef.

Pots and Pans

You'll need something to cook in, whether that's an expensive, ultralight nesting set for backcountry travel or a used saucepan you picked up at a garage sale. Be warned that if you bring your nice pans from home and use them over an open fire, you may find yourself scrubbing for a long time to get the black soot stains off the bottom. Basic pots like the MSR Ceramic 2-Pot Set are inexpensive, work in car-camping and backcountry settings, and will last for years.

Plates/Bowls

If you're by yourself, you can eat right out of the pot if you want to (and then you only have to wash one dish!). But a plastic, aluminum, or titanium bowl

and/or plate can be nice, depending on what you're cooking. Avoid glass: It's heavy, and broken glass at a campsite is never cool—or easy to clean up.

Flatware

The minimalist will tell you that you can do everything with a single spoon, but if weight and bulk aren't a consideration (i.e., you're not going into the backcountry), knock yourself out and bring the whole flatware set. Just make sure you have something long enough to use to stir inside a big pot.

Water Container

If you're certain your campground has water available, you can buy a couple one-gallon plastic jugs full of water at a grocery store and refill them at the campground. Or you can purchase a five- or seven-gallon plastic jug at an outdoor store to refill and reuse every time you go camping. These are nice options also because you don't have to refill the jugs as often as with smaller containers. For backpacking, you usually won't need to carry more than 2 or 3 liters at a time, so you can use a couple of water bottles or a large reservoir like the MSR Dromedary bag.

Camp Chair

If you're fine with sitting on sometimes-damp rocks and logs (or don't anticipate having a lot of downtime), you can omit a camp chair. But if you plan on some solid sitting time around a campfire or expect to take a day to chill at a campsite, a chair is advisable. Technology and bright design minds have delivered us compact, sub-one-pound camp chairs for backcountry travel, but any fifteen-dollar camp chair from an outdoor store (or even a grocery store) will do the trick for any other type of camping.

Hatchet

To build a campfire at a car-camping site, a basic hatchet is a must—not a huge ax, just a simple, one-handed wood splitter. It'll help you chop the logs you picked up at the 7-Eleven near the campground into smaller pieces that will actually burn (most states don't want you to transport firewood over state lines due to insect and disease transfer issues).

Lighter

A cheap lighter from a convenience store will do, both for lighting your stove and lighting your campfire. (Not a bad idea to bring two of them, just in case.)

Backpacking, quite simply, means camping with more solitude, more stars, and a more immersive experience in nature. You will rarely, if ever, find a backpacking campsite interrupted by the headlights of a car or the music from a neighboring campsite (situations that can happen when car camping). In the backcountry, you'll encounter fewer people, too. But you'll see more stars and more uninterrupted panoramas because you're farther from the lights of a city or town. The deeper you get into wilderness, away from civilization, the more you fully experience nature—moose, old-growth pines, pristine mountain streams. Being absorbed in nature can give you a pretty wonderful feeling. It might surprise you.

Setting up camp in Cumberland Island National Seashore

If you haven't done it before, backpacking probably seems like a lot of work: Gather all the food and gear you need to survive for a few days in the wilderness, load it into a backpack, then throw that big, heavy pack on your shoulders and walk for miles until you find a campsite.

Well, I've got good news for you: Yes, backpacking actually *is* work, whether you've done it before or not. But two things make it easier: first, knowing that in the end, the experience is worth the effort, and second, learning to pack only what you need so your backpack is less heavy. (Spoiler alert: The pack will probably always feel heavy, no matter how minimally you pack. Unless you forget to pack one or two important things, in which case it will feel eerily light.)

Backpacking isn't rocket science. You don't necessarily need fancy equipment. Sure, it's nice to have an ultralight tent and sleeping bag, but that's not required. You can tie any sleeping bag or tent to the outside of a pack. If you're hiking with a friend, you may be able to share some of the load.

Also, you don't have to hike ten miles into the backcountry to have a good time. Even if you hike only two miles from the parking lot before you set up your tent, you're still backpacking. Yes, the farther from the parking lot you travel, the more solitude you'll gain, but if you hike into the backcountry at all, you'll quickly notice how few camping neighbors you have.

Popular Destinations

Bright Angel Trail (Grand Canyon National Park). A nine-mile hike dropping 4,500 vertical feet to the campground at the bottom of the Grand Canyon, the Bright Angel Trail is a popular two- or three-day backpacking trip—if you can snag a permit for it.

Appalachian Trail (Georgia to Maine). Can't quit your job to thru-hike the entire Appalachian Trail? Do a section of it at a time. Plenty of great scenery along the 2,191-mile AT can be accessed in two- or three-day trips.

John Muir Trail (California). Definitely not a beginner's trail, the 210-mile JMT is a life-list goal for many backpackers, featuring three weeks of hiking in the Sierra Nevada.

Teton Crest Trail (Wyoming). A forty-mile route through the heart of the Tetons, this trail crosses several high passes with nearly constant views of craggy peaks.

Long Trail (Vermont). This 272-mile trail was America's first long-distance hiking trail, and like the AT, you can tackle it in pieces. Lots of shorter options exist on this path that summits many of the highest Green Mountain peaks.

Chicago Basin (Colorado). Take the Durango & Silverton Narrow Gauge Railroad into the San Juan Mountains to access this alpine lake basin, from which you can hike to the top of one (or several) 14,000-foot peaks.

W Trek (Torres del Paine National Park, Chile). This five-day, four-night trip is one of the world's most famous, a marquee tour of the glaciers and towering peaks of one of Patagonia's most photographed national parks.

A "bear hang"—hanging food in a tree out of reach of bears—works on a smaller scale in non-bear territory. In this case, campers hang their food, toiletries, and cookware in stuff sacks to keep them out of reach of industrious squirrels and opossum.

Cooking a one-pot meal on a small backpacking stove. Stoves are useful and efficient for cooking even when you have a campfire.

Gear

Mummy-style sleeping bag. Unlike your duvet at home, bigger is not better when it comes to sleeping bags. Over the past half century, lighter, more compact sleeping bag designs have revolutionized backpacking, and you'll be pleasantly surprised how comfortable you can be on a freezing night when you zip into something that takes up less space than a hotel pillow.

Packable sleeping pad. This won't remind you of the pillow-top mattress you have at home, but it will be way more comfortable than sleeping on the hard ground, and it will weigh less than two pounds.

Headlamp. Very simply, this is a lightweight flashlight you wear on your head, so you can use both hands to do things, like cook, set up tents, and organize your gear.

Lightweight tent. On a backpacking trip, you can carry a spacious tent that weighs twelve pounds or a compact tent that weighs four. Although you might feel a little cramped at first in a lightweight tent, one trip carrying a twelve-pound tent on your back should cure you of that mild claustrophobia.

Backpacking stove. A lightweight, compact, single-burner stove often takes up less space than a can of beer. No one wants to carry a big, heavy, two-burner car-camping stove in a pack.

Backpacking trowel. Shaped like your gardening trowel at home (but much more lightweight), this is used to dig catholes to bury human waste in the backcountry—both a rite of passage and a conservation measure to ensure we all enjoy our backpacking trips and don't have to step in each other's . . . you know, shit.

Top: A backpacker cinches down the straps on their pack before beginning the day's hike. **Above Right:** Clothes dry on a log after swimming/laundry time. **Right:** A gravity water filter hangs from a tree, ready to be filtered.

Above: An angler steps out of an alpine lake after trying their luck just before sunset. **Left:** A sign advises backpackers that they are entering an active bear habitat and that all food and toiletries must be kept in secure, hard-sided bear canisters.

Pack a Backpack

Your first few efforts packing a backpack will be trial and error as you figure out your own personal system, but in general, you should strive to load your pack in the following order: First, in the bottom of the pack, put the lightweight objects you won't need during the day: sleeping bag, sleeping pad (if it fits inside the pack), and tent. On top of that, stow the heavy stuff (extra water, dinner and breakfast food, stove, fuel, cookware) so that the heaviest items sit right up against your back. Then, on top of that, stash things you'll need quick access to: snacks for the day, extra layers you might need (like a rain jacket), and a water bottle (if your pack lacks an exterior bottle pocket). Once you've established that basic structure, take your extra clothes and slide them into crevices in the pack, evenly filling all the spaces down below with them. When you put the pack on, it shouldn't list to one side or pull you backward—if it does, repack so the contents are more centered, keeping the heaviest things as close as possible to the middle of the pack and near your back.

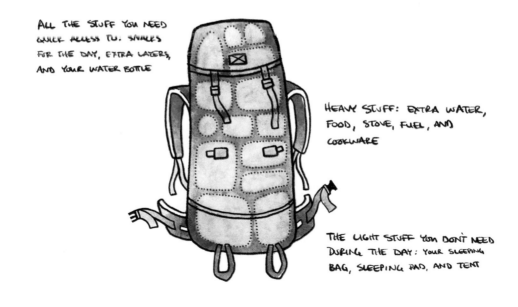

ALL THE STUFF YOU NEED QUICK ACCESS TO: SNACKS FOR THE DAY, EXTRA LAYERS, AND YOUR WATER BOTTLE

HEAVY STUFF: EXTRA WATER, FOOD, STOVE, FUEL, AND COOKWARE

THE LIGHT STUFF YOU DON'T NEED DURING THE DAY: YOUR SLEEPING BAG, SLEEPING PAD, AND TENT

TEN TIPS FOR CAMPING WITH YOUR DOG

Why not bring your best buddy on your next outdoor adventure? If you do a little preparation, you can ensure a good time for both of you.

1) Schedule a veterinarian visit beforehand to make sure your dog is up-to-date on vaccinations. Ask about medications for fleas, ticks, and heartworms, too.

2) Research dog-friendly campsites before you go (plenty of US national parks allow dogs in campgrounds, but not on trails inside the park).

3) Bring a leash, a tie-out cable, and a stake. Some campgrounds require dogs to be on a leash at all times, and you'll want to be able to have your hands free at least some of the time.

4) Take one portable bowl for water and one for food—collapsible dog-specific ones, or just a couple of old plastic containers.

5) If you're hiking, pack extra food and make sure your dog eats and drinks.

6) Remember to bring poop bags. When you're hiking, don't forget to take the full poop bags back with you.

7) Pack a few dog-specific first-aid items (tweezers and/or needle-nose pliers for removing thorns, quills, or spines; a booty for an injured paw; a basic dog first-aid book).

8) Decide on sleeping arrangements before you head out. Will your dog sleep in the tent with you? Will he fit in your sleeping bag? (An old child-size sleeping bag can work great for a dog.)

9) If you're backpacking, check your dog's paws every day to make sure they're okay (she won't tell you when her paws are hurting).

10) If you're in bear country, keep your dog on a leash at all times. Note that even outside of bear country, lots of wilderness areas require dogs to be leashed at all times.

"MAY YOUR TRAILS BE CROOKED, WINDING, LONESOME, DANGEROUS, LEADING TO THE MOST AMAZING VIEW. MAY YOUR MOUNTAINS RISE INTO AND ABOVE THE CLOUDS. IT IS NOT ENOUGH TO FIGHT FOR THE LAND; IT IS EVEN MORE IMPORTANT TO ENJOY IT. WHILE YOU CAN."

—EDWARD ABBEY,
DESERT SOLITAIRE

Above: Ideal sleeping quarters are found in this designated, well-established campsite; it comes with a fire ring and plenty of natural seating options used by prior campers. **Right:** A hammock can be a great addition to a campsite for overnight sleeping or lounging and napping—just make sure it's attached to sturdy trees.

Pick Out a Backcountry Campsite

There's one main guideline when camping in the backcountry: You should *find* a campsite, not make one. Unless you're bushwhacking in the jungle (you're not), you should be able to locate a spot large enough for a tent, one that doesn't require chopping through brush, breaking off or cutting tree limbs, or stamping down grass or plants. The best campsite is one that has been previously used—preferably by lots of people. It will be flat (or flat enough) and have a somewhat bare spot where tents have been pitched many times in recent years, and most of the rocks that would jut into the floor of your tent will have already been relocated by prior campers. To determine if a site is flat, simply eyeball it. Or you can physically lie down in the spot to test it; do you feel like you'll slide downhill or roll one way or another during the night? If yes, keep looking. Additionally, you want enough room for any doors and vestibules (and for you to get out of the tent without whacking your head on a tree branch). Finally, your tent site should be at least two hundred feet from lakes and streams. You may need to hunt for a campsite, yet if you know what to look for, it should be easy to find a pre-established site meeting these criteria in all but the most remote areas.

200 FEET

Am I Doing This Right?

Carry something a little heavy—say, two cans of beer or a can of chili or a five-hundred-page paperback book—with you eight or ten miles into the backcountry, and more than one person might question your judgment. You might question your own judgment, too, depending on how sweaty and tired you are by the time you get to camp and open that beer, or chili, or paperback.

Just as there are a million opinions on how to live, there are a million approaches to camping. It's easy to wonder at times: *Am I doing this right?*

Answer: *Yes.* As long as you are having fun, not disturbing other people, and not dying, you're doing it right. Cram a superheavy, bulky air mattress into a giant tent that sprawls over an entire campsite. Or sleep on an ultrathin foam pad in a sub-three-pound tent in a sliver of ground between two slickrock benches. If you enjoy it, it's okay—even if it's the complete opposite of what you see other people doing. And it probably will be the complete opposite of what other people are doing.

There's a famous saying in the climbing world, by the late alpinist Alex Lowe: "The best climber in the world is the one having the most fun." This is a sentiment that can, and should, be applied to every leisure pursuit in your life. Don't worry about what other people are doing—just focus on doing what makes you happy.

When you're camping at a large campground, you will see people with bigger tents, smaller tents, no tents, fancy stoves, tiny stoves, big vans, stylish tow-behind trailers, RVs the size of city buses; maybe even people who bicycled there with all their gear strapped to their bikes. You can learn a lot just from casually observing the people at nearby campsites, even more if you strike up a conversation about their camping setup or where they're from.

From brand-new six-figure RVs to road-battered touring bikes with minimalist camping gear, no one's right or wrong—just different. Although on a cold night walking back to your tent as the frost settles in, it's easy to find yourself looking longingly into the window of an RV, where the people inside play cards or read books as a space heater runs, and wonder how comfortable they are.

Of course, camping is not always about being comfortable. If it were, we might never go.

If you want a quiet night sleeping under the stars—
a really, really quiet night—snow camping is for you.
Go a little ways into the backcountry on a pair of
snowshoes or skis and set up a tent. Solitude is almost
a guarantee.

The goal in snow camping is to prepare before your trip so that you bring
all the necessities (like a shovel, plenty of stove fuel, a sleeping bag rated to
zero degree Fahrenheit, and a warm down jacket), to keep your hands and
feet warm enough, and to give yourself plenty of time for things like cooking
dinner and setting up camp before darkness all too quickly sets in.

Few people camp in the snow just for the sheer joy (or semimisery) of
camping in the snow. Most do as part of a different goal, like climbing Denali
in Alaska or Mount Shasta in California or skiing in the backcountry. Once
you learn how to camp in a snowy environment, all sorts of opportunities
open up to you. As longtime National Outdoor Leadership School instructor
and climber Steve Goryl said while preparing for a 1994 climb of Mount
Everest, "It's just camping."

If you look at a photo of a tent in the snow and think, *That looks miserable*,
well, lots of people would say you're at least half correct. For starters, snow
camping usually is *cold*. You have to melt snow to get water to cook with and
drink. You wear gloves most of the time. If it's snowing heavily, you might
have to get up in the night to shovel snow off the top of the tent so you don't
suffocate inside it. You won't usually find a rock, log, or any other surface to
set your stuff down on—but with some shoveling, you can build yourself
a chair or a table. Also, if the snow isn't consolidated, you might posthole up
to your knee or higher every time you take a step away from your tent (like if
you're getting up in the middle of the night when nature calls).

Camping in the snow typically requires different gear than you'd take for,
say, a summer backpacking trip. Warmer sleeping bags, tents with less mesh
on the walls, and in general warmer clothing make the experience more
comfortable and safer. Basic avalanche knowledge is a necessity for trips in
the mountains, even in well-traveled or popular routes. And, of course, since
trails are invisible when they're covered in a few feet of snow, navigation is
a completely different challenge in the winter.

You certainly can pitch a tent in the snow without having a mountaineering
or skiing objective. Simply pick a spot a mile or two from a trailhead and
spend a night out there for fun. Or "fun," as might be.

Gear

Mountaineering tent. Mountaineering tents are similar to regular backpacking tents but are beefed up structurally, usually with less mesh on the tent body walls. They often have two doors to allow you to cook just inside the vestibule and set up a cross-breeze so your stove doesn't consume all the oxygen in your tent and suffocate you (this is a real danger). Many outdoor gear stores rent mountaineering tents for winter camping—a far less committing way to try it out than buying a tent at full price.

Shovel. A collapsible avalanche shovel is pretty much a necessity for scooping out a platform for your tent and a necessary piece of your avalanche kit if you're traveling in the mountains between November and May.

Zero-degree sleeping bag. A typical three-season sleeping bag is rated somewhere between fifteen and thirty-two degrees Fahrenheit, which means it will probably keep you reasonably warm down to a temperature about ten degrees above that. If you're camping in temperatures of thirty degrees or lower, you'll want a sleeping bag rated to zero degree or lower.

Pee bottle/FUD. A pee bottle is simply an old water bottle you designate for urine so you don't have to get out of your tent in the middle of the night. Clearly label it so you don't mistake it for your water bottle. An FUD (feminine urinary device) enables women to use a pee bottle as well, and many women swear by this tool in plenty of situations, not just snow camping. A bit of home practice is advised before utilizing one inside a tent for the first time.

Puffy jacket. Nothing packs more warmth per weight than good old-fashioned goose down, and a legit winter puffy jacket will become your best friend in cold temperatures. Yes, you'll look a little like the Michelin Man in it, but when it's that cold outside and you're warm inside your puffy jacket, you won't care.

Left: A backpack, stiff-soled mountaineering boots, and quick-drying, lightweight warm layers sit to the side as a campsite is established in the snow. **Below:** An avalanche beacon (as well as the training to know how to use it) is a must for traveling in avalanche terrain for snow camping. **Bottom:** Two people dig and stomp out a snowy platform for their sleep and cook tents on a glacier.

Popular Destinations

Mount Shasta (California). This is one of the most popular volcano climbs in the Lower 48. Every weekend during the climbing season (usually May and June), the camp at Helen Lake, 10,443 feet, is full of climbers camping there and heading for the summit the following morning.

Mount Adams (Washington). A great first volcano climb just north of the Washington-Oregon border, Mount Adams draws many first-time snow climbers, who split the 6,676-foot climb into two days by pitching a tent somewhere partway up the South Spur route.

Mount Whitney (California). The Mountaineers Route, a technical climb to the summit of the highest peak in the Lower 48, is best climbed when spring snow is still present on the route, which means camping on snow somewhere partway up the mountain.

Presidential Traverse (New Hampshire). The winter Presidential Traverse is a rite of passage for many mountaineers and is considered a solid training outing for mountains like Rainier or Denali. Even during a good-weather window, this route is cold and very serious, and requires at least two nights of snow camping. During a bad-weather window, well, it's just not a good idea.

Top: Lightweight sun protection is important while camping in snow—UV rays come from above as well as bounce off the snow beneath you. **Bottom Left:** Most (and almost all) water used for drinking and cooking on a snow camping trip comes from melting the abundant snow surrounding camp. **Bottom Right:** Skiers fill out summit permits at a trailhead for a popular ski mountaineering excursion.

Above: Expedition members carry gear from a bush plane to establish their camp on a glacier. **Left:** A climber works to anchor the cook tent with a snow bollard.

"IT'S JUST CAMPING."

—STEVE GORYL
(ROBERT BIRKBY, *MOUNTAIN MADNESS:
MT. EVEREST AND THE LIFE
& LEGACY OF SCOTT FISCHER*)

Make a Deadman Anchor

If you pound a tent stake into snow using the technique you use in dirt, you'll almost surely be disappointed by the results: The stability offered by tent stakes in snow is usually only a few percentage points better than having no stakes at all, because snow is so soft. Thankfully, there's a solution, and it's simple: Once you know where you want to stake your tent, (1) dig a small hole where you'd normally drive in a stake—around six inches deep. (2) Put a tent stake through the tie-down webbing or guyline, and lay the stake down in the hole so it's lying parallel with the ground. (3) Then, pack snow back into the hole until it's firm, covering the stake, (4) and compact the snow with your boot sole, if you can. Wait a couple minutes, and the new snow should be frozen in place, holding the tent firmly. (If it hasn't frozen, you may have to wait until evening to stake the tent, when the temperature has decreased a little bit so the snow can refreeze.) Repeat the process for your other tie-downs and guylines and you'll have a stable tent setup.

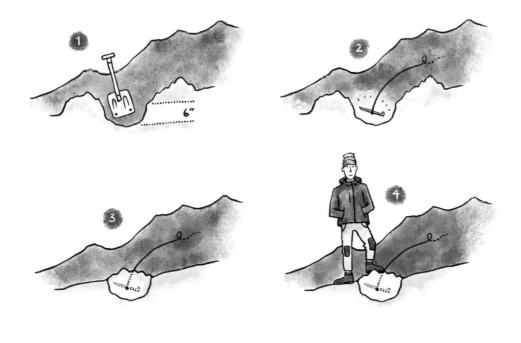

Left: A skier fills their bottle with freshly melted water made from snow. **Below:** Sunscreen is a must-carry item on a snow-camping trip. **Bottom:** A well-dug "kitchen" provides a cooking "counter" as well as benches for sitting and enough room to stand up underneath the tarp.

A Brief History of Recreational Camping in the United States

How long have humans been camping? Well, you could say we've been doing it forever, since living indoors didn't really become a thing until a few thousand years ago, and everything humans did up until that point was essentially camping. Our ancestors who lived in caves? Camping, if you think about it. The Ancestral Puebloans, who disappeared only a few hundred years ago and whose cliff dwellings still stand in the desert Southwest? They pretty much were campers, by our standards.

Contemporary camping—where we leave our comfortable homes and spend a night or a few out in nature—hasn't been a pastime for long. It became common in the mid-1800s, and its explosion in popularity is usually traced to the publication in 1869 of an unexpected bestseller. William H. H. Murray's *Adventures in the Wilderness* was a breakthrough in outdoor literature, combining romantic descriptions of the wild terrain of New York's Adirondack Mountains with plenty of detailed info on how city dwellers of the northeastern United States could do it themselves. Camping historian Terence Young, in his book *Heading Out: A History of American Camping*, called Murray's book "the watershed book in the history of American camping" and explained how sales of the book brought thousands of visitors to a then-sleepy region during the summer of 1869.

Murray's writing was unique at the time in encouraging women to adventure in the outdoors, and more than a few did, including Kate Field, who planned a camping trip to the Adirondacks during July 1869 with three other women—and no men were invited. By late 1869, Field was delivering lectures on how women could camp by themselves, without men, and drawing crowds along with a bit of pushback from a few stodgy fellows who considered the outdoors to be man's domain. During 1869 and the following years, taking summer holidays in the wilderness became tremendously popular, thanks to Murray's book.

Murray didn't invent camping, of course—he just wrote about it in a way that inspired thousands to follow in his footsteps. The YWCA and YMCA both started their first summer camps for women and men in the subsequent years—the YWCA in 1874 in Asbury Park, New Jersey, and the YMCA a decade later in 1885, at Lake Orange, New York. They weren't the first summer camps, however: Many historians point to Frederick Gunn, an educator who in 1861 took forty-two of his students (thirty boys and twelve girls) on a thirty-mile trek from Washington, Connecticut, to a point on Long Island Sound, where they camped for ten days. This was during the height of the Civil War, which, as a side effect, was teaching thousands of men camping skills that they could use after the war.

The early 1900s saw the birth of both the Girl Scouts and Boy Scouts, both drawing inspiration from Brit Robert Baden-Powell's Girl Guides and Boy Scouts. The Boy Scouts of America was founded in 1910 and set up their first official camp at Silver Bay on Lake George, New York. The Girl Scouts were founded in Savannah, Georgia, in 1912 and established their first official camp in 1913, on nearby Wassaw Island.

All this was happening as Americans were beginning to recognize the need to preserve and protect wild places. Yellowstone National Park, America's first national park, was established in 1872; Mackinac Island National Park, the second national park, was established in 1875. Yosemite National Park followed in 1890, and the first national monument, Devils Tower National Monument, was established in 1906. In 1916 the National Park Service was created to manage America's growing park system. States began managing park areas in 1825, but none officially called them state parks until 1895, when Michigan's Mackinac Island National Park became Mackinac Island State Park.

In 1933, the National Industrial Recovery Act authorized the creation of the Federal Emergency Administration of Public Works to administer a program of public works projects to conserve and develop natural resources—which laid the foundation for the federal government to purchase land for recreation. The program developed, among its forty-six projects in more than twenty states, campgrounds within reach of major urban areas. In November 1936, the projects were transferred to the National Park Service, and in 1937, thirty-one of the completed campgrounds (out of sixty-four) received one hundred thousand camper-days use. By 1941, a hundred organized campgrounds across the country had been finished and were being heavily used. The campgrounds were later turned over to states and cities to be managed, and in the 1930s, through that process and other federal job-creation programs, more than eight hundred state parks were created.

By the mid-1900s, the groundwork had been laid to make public lands accessible, and the relative affluence of the post–World War II years enabled hundreds of thousands of Americans to escape their cities and spend holidays in nature.

Imagine packing for a camping trip and taking anything you want with you: a six-burner stove, steaks, beer, camp chairs, tables, coolers full of fruit and vegetables, and your guitar. Then, imagine you and your friends have an entire riverfront campground to yourselves every night—but you never stay in the same spot. Each day, you get up and move your camp to a different riverfront campsite, riding the roller coaster of white water to get there. Did I mention there's a toilet? There is. With an actual toilet seat. Oh, and you'll sleep under the stars every night, often with the sound of rushing water nearby—which drowns out any snoring friends.

River enthusiasts know how to do a lot of things, but one of the things they do best is camp. Multiday whitewater raft trips are probably the most luxurious self-supported camping you can experience in the real backcountry—far from power outlets, faucets, flush toilets, and cell phone signals. Your vehicle is an eighteen-foot whitewater raft with more storage than most cars. The only caveat is whatever you bring has to be in a waterproof container, just in case the raft flips in a rapid—because that can happen.

To take a whitewater raft trip, you have two options: Sign up for a commercial guided trip (more expensive, but much less planning and effort on your part), or go with a private, unguided trip (more planning, gear, logistics, and knowledge involved, plus you're rowing the raft yourself). If you don't have a group of friends who are experienced with whitewater rafting—not only rowing rafts, but also organizing groups, rigging boats, planning food for a large group of people, and lining up permits—you'll want to take a guided trip.

Guided whitewater raft trips are as short as a quick overnight (one night of camping and two days of rafting) and as long as two weeks (which you can find in the Grand Canyon). Private trips can be as long as twenty-eight days (which is the longest permitted winter trip in the Grand Canyon; you need more days on the river to make up for the short amount of daylight). Regardless of which route you choose, your days will be punctuated with big rapids, with stretches of calmer water in between. Expect a lot of downtime to hike and explore terrain by foot, which is the real joy of whitewater trips for many people.

You'll have a hearty breakfast in the morning, pack up everything to head down the river, stop somewhere along the water for lunch, pick a campsite for the evening, then have dinner and drinks, perhaps next to a campfire.

River trips, like all other properly executed camping trips, follow the principles of Leave No Trace—you pack it in, you pack it out, and you leave the campsite better than you found it. This includes removing the ashes from any campfires you make along the way. All raft trips are required to carry a fire pan to remove ashes, as well as a "groover," a portable toilet with tanks that enable you to haul all solid human waste with you. Yes, that's slightly gross, but imagine all ten thousand people who raft through the Grand Canyon every year trying to dig holes and bury their stuff near the beach campsites—it would quickly turn into a toxic-waste nightmare. Look on the bright side: You get to sit down every morning on an actual toilet seat and enjoy the scenery of the river while you do your thing.

All those creature comforts—the chairs and tables, big stoves, great food, coolers, and even the groover—make a "roughing it" trip not as rough, and that's the good news. The less good news is that someone has to haul all that fun stuff from the boats to the campsite every night, and vice versa every morning. If you're on a private, nonguided trip, that means you'll be hauling it, but if you're on a guided trip, the guide staff will do most of the heavy work—you'll just be responsible for taking down your tent and packing your gear every morning. Something to consider if you're weighing the private versus guided trip question.

"REAL FREEDOM LIES IN WILDNESS,
NOT IN CIVILIZATION."

—CHARLES LINDBERGH
(A. SCOTT BERG, *LINDBERGH*)

Popular Destinations

Colorado River through the Grand Canyon (Arizona; ten to sixteen days). This is arguably the granddaddy of multiday rafting trips in the United States—millions of people see the Grand Canyon from the rim every year, but only a few thousand view it from the river.

Gates of Lodore (Colorado/Utah; three to four days). A shorter, but no less striking, desert river trip through Dinosaur National Monument in western Colorado and eastern Utah.

Yampa River (Colorado/Utah; four to five days). Beginning in northern Colorado and then joining the Green River, the Yampa is one of the most sought-after trips in the West for its desert scenery.

Middle Fork of the Salmon River (Idaho; six days). One hundred whitewater rapids in a hundred miles, plus natural hot springs and mountain views.

Rogue River (Oregon; three to five days). Less intense rafting on more mellow white water, with views of gorges and waterfalls, and plenty of calm water.

Cataract Canyon (Utah; six days). A remote, exciting section of the Colorado River through Utah's Canyon Country, containing a fourteen-mile section of whitewater rapids rated up to Class V (see page 62).

Zambezi River (Zimbabwe; three to four days). Nicknamed the Slam-bezi for its fun, roller-coaster big-water rapids, the Zambezi sports some of the world's most legendary whitewater rafting. Several companies guide multiday trips on the river, with beach camping.

Gear

Dry bags. Roll-top, watertight bags made of polyurethane-coated fabric to keep your extra clothes and gear dry through splashing rapids and even submersion if a raft flips and your stuff goes underwater.

Watertight cases. Hard plastic cases will keep more fragile gear (like cameras and lenses) dry and guarded from impact in the event of a raft flipping.

Paco pads. Thick, waterproof, durable camping pads made of coated fabric, these may be the most comfortable pads you'll ever sleep on, and they double as seat pads while rafting.

Water shoes/sandals. Your feet will get wet no matter what shoes you wear rafting, so your footwear might as well let water pass through. Strappy sandals like those made by Chaco and Teva have been favorites for many years, but more substantial water shoes with toe protection have started to gain popularity.

PFD. The personal floatation device, or a "life jacket," is required pretty much anywhere you could fall off a boat and into rushing water.

Groover. The portable toilet required on all raft trips, so the river doesn't turn into everyone's toilet (*ewww*).

River sandals are built to hike on sandy and rocky terrain, and they drain well when they get wet.

The gear on a rafting trip gets packed into watertight dry bags.

Top: A boat captain unloads a bundle of driftwood gathered during the day's rafting. **Above:** A raft expedition member stamps letters and postcards for mules to carry from the river to civilization, and eventually, the post office. **Right:** Two boaters prepare to meet their destiny as they enter an exciting rapid.

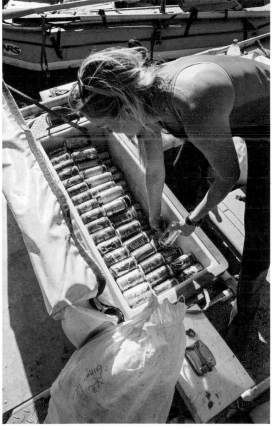

Above: An expedition leader studies the river map for the day's journey downriver to the next camp. **Left:** A boat captain stocks a cooler with beverages.

THE INTERNATIONAL SCALE OF RIVER DIFFICULTY

Water conditions on rivers will vary, depending on where you travel, but this list explains how the American Whitewater organization classifies rapids.

Class I: Easy. Fast-moving water with riffles and small waves. Few obstructions, all obvious and easily missed with little training. Risk to swimmers is slight; self-rescue is easy.

Class II: Novice. Straightforward rapids with wide, clear channels that are evident without scouting. Occasional maneuvering may be required, but rocks and medium-size waves are easily missed by trained paddlers. Swimmers are seldom injured, and group assistance, while helpful, is seldom needed.

Class III: Intermediate. Rapids with moderate, irregular waves that may be difficult to avoid and that can swamp an open canoe. Complex maneuvers in fast currents and good boat control in tight passages or around ledges are often required; large waves or strainers may be present but are easily avoided. Strong eddies and powerful current effects can be found, particularly on large-volume rivers. Scouting is advisable for inexperienced parties. Injuries while swimming are rare; self-rescue is usually easy, but group assistance may be required to avoid long swims.

Class IV: Advanced. Intense, powerful, but predictable rapids requiring precise boat handling in turbulent water. Depending on the character of the river, it may feature large, unavoidable waves and holes or constricted passages demanding fast maneuvers under pressure. A fast, reliable eddy turn may be needed to initiate maneuvers, scout rapids, or rest. Rapids may require "must" moves above dangerous hazards. Scouting may be necessary the first time down. Risk of injury to swimmers is moderate to high, and water conditions may make self-rescue difficult. Group assistance for rescue is often essential but requires practiced skills. A strong Eskimo roll is highly recommended.

Class V: Expert. Extremely long, obstructed, or very violent rapids that expose a paddler to added risk. Drops may contain large, unavoidable waves and holes or steep, congested chutes with complex, demanding routes. Rapids may continue for long distances between pools, demanding a high level of fitness. What eddies exist may be small, turbulent, or difficult to reach. At the high end of the scale, several of these factors may be combined. Scouting is recommended but may be difficult. Swims are dangerous, and rescue is often difficult even for experts. A very reliable Eskimo roll, proper equipment, extensive experience, and practiced rescue skills are essential.

Above: An inflatable stand-up paddleboard provides a means for exploring a quiet side canyon on a raft trip. **Right:** Taking some downtime at the riverside campsite.

Pack a Dry Bag

Dry bags are simple but magical inventions, and there's one main rule when packing them: Don't overpack. Dry bags have one opening, at the top, and if the bag is too full to seal that opening, the interior may not stay dry and you might ruin or lose some of your stuff. So it's a good idea to test pack a dry bag before your rafting or kayaking trip to make sure you have plenty of room to seal it properly. If you can't seal the bag, figure out what items you need to place in another bag or leave behind.

When packing a dry bag: Maximize the amount of stuff in the bottom of the bag and minimize the air in the bag. Sounds simple, but if you have a narrow dry bag, it can be difficult to cram a sleeping bag into it, for example. (Solution: Take the sleeping bag out of its stuff sack and feed the sleeping bag into the dry bag a few inches at a time.) Once your gear is in the dry bag, leave the end of the dry bag open and squeeze as much air out as you can. Then, roll the top down and fold it at least three times before you buckle the bag.

You'll likely pack your stuff in several dry bags, including a small one to hold the things you'll need during the day, such as snacks, a camera, a water bottle, and sunscreen.

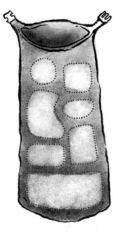
MAKE SURE ALL YOUR BELONGINGS EASILY FIT IN THE BAG.

SQUEEZE OUT ALL THE EXTRA AIR FROM THE BAG AND ROLL THE TOP DOWN.

BUCKLE THE TOP TO SECURE.

A Slight Reality Check

You've seen those perfect Instagram camping photos, the ones in which the campers have woken up with their tent doors opening to perfectly lit, pristine mountains or coastal scenes, maybe while they sip coffee and stare off into the distance, thinking about how endless the universe is and how small they are in it. Here's the thing about those snapshots: You can't photograph smells. Another thing: The light is only perfect for a few minutes, an hour if you're lucky. To capture the perfect moment—sipping java, bathed in golden light with the perfect view—you have to get up early to make the coffee. And no matter how plush the sleeping bag looks, there's a solid chance that it has at least a whiff of BO—and that it's not as comfy as a king-size bed with fresh linens at the Hyatt.

Camping is great, but there's a reason it's called "roughing it." To get those sunrises and sunsets and unimpeded views of stars, you have to sacrifice a few things. Running water and a flushing toilet in the next room, for example. Actually, you're sacrificing the next room, because there are no rooms. If you want hot food or coffee, you'll have to cook it yourself, on a stove with one to three burners fewer than the appliance you have at home. If you're cold, there's no thermostat to turn up—you'll have to build a campfire or layer on more clothing. Whatever sleeping pad you're using, it's not as soft as your pillow-top mattress at home. And there might be some mosquitoes.

But all of this is okay. You're trading a few home comforts for things you can't replicate at home: The fragrance of a deep forest of pine trees. Cool morning moments without the noise or smell of nearby traffic. A sky full of stars unimpeded by the fog of urban light pollution. The ineffable calm generated by staring into the embers at the base of a campfire (instead of a glowing phone screen or television). The tang of wood smoke in your nose and clothes. And maybe the best of all, the freedom from having to look presentable in any way, because you're camping and no one expects you to have showered or be wearing fresh clothes.

If you're new to camping (and even if you're a long-timer), you may experience a moment or two when you say to yourself, "Sleeping in a tent sure looks a lot different on Instagram." And you'd be right. Your weekend in the woods may not look or feel like those staged photos, but it will be better than Instagram in countless other ways.

Car camping (a euphemism for "campsites you can drive to in any type of motor vehicle") has probably the lowest barrier to entry. You don't need a fancy, state-of-the-art, superlightweight tent—any tent that keeps you dry in the rain will do. You can skip the three-hundred-dollar sleeping bag (although it might be nice). You don't have to hike into the backcountry to find a campsite—if you live in the continental United States, you likely live within a few dozen miles of a campground or a state or county park with campsites available for around twenty bucks per night.

Car camping is undoubtedly the most comfortable way to camp. You're limited only by the size of your car's trunk, or the bed of your pickup, or the back of your minivan, so you can bring almost whatever you want. Want to bring your pillow from home? You can. Your favorite skillet for making omelettes? Absolutely. A cooler full of steaks? Sure thing (just make sure there's a grill where you're going, or tote one yourself). Your fifty-inch flat-screen TV for watching the game? Well, let's not get carried away. But within reason, you can pretty much bring anything.

Car camping enables you to see the world in remarkable ways. For one, it immerses you in places you might not have access to if you stayed in a hotel— the wild interior of Denali National Park in Alaska, for one example, or the alpine lakes of Rocky Mountain National Park in Colorado. Yes, you can stay in a hotel near those parks, but you won't see a sunset every night from the interior of a hotel room or feel the cool morning air in the trees and smell the dew on the brush as you rise from your tent. Second, car camping can make long road trips financially feasible, especially in areas where dispersed camping is free (such as in some US Forest Service and Bureau of Land Management lands in the western United States). A seven-day road trip can get expensive if you stay in a hotel every night. But if you stay in a twenty-dollar campsite each night along the way, your adventure can be signficantly less expensive. Simply learn how to make yourself at home in a tent and sleeping bag, and the world is your oyster.

A vehicle packed to capacity with car camping supplies: a stove, tents, pots, firewood, water, food, and fuel.

Packing a cooler with ice is important but keeping it in the shade can keep it cool much longer than in the sun.

Of course, you don't have to travel long distances. Driving a few miles from your home to spend a night or two under the stars can be a refreshing experience. Even without a great physical distance, the psychological distance from all the things on your mind back at home can be significant. Work, house projects, bills, schedules, laundry—these can easily fade into the background during an evening sitting around a campfire. The beauty of camping is in its simplicity: You're brought back to a basic way of living. It might be less convenient and less comfortable to be without running water, a fancy stove and oven, and lights that turn on via a switch on a wall or a tap on a phone, but camping will refocus you on the basics of survival, and that process of simplification can be very relaxing. You have one choice for breakfast, one option for dinner, zero cable channels to distract you, and no daunting chores to worry about.

Car camping requires no special skills other than packing the trunk. It doesn't have to be an epic adventure to be worthwhile. Get a sleeping bag to keep you warm, a sleeping pad of some sort to keep you comfortable through the night, a tent to keep you dry, and maybe a chair to sit in while you read or watch the sun set, and you're pretty much ready to go. Do it in your backyard, at the campground down the street, in the neighboring state, or halfway across the country. The glorious choice is yours.

Gear

Roll-up table. Plenty of car-camping sites have picnic tables, but if you're hunting out your own dispersed campsite, a roll-up table is an underrated luxury, providing a flat surface for preparing and/or cooking food.

Camp chairs. A decent fold-up camp chair from any discount store can be worth its weight in gold around a campfire. Whether you spend fifteen dollars or fifty, you'll be excited to have something other than a tree stump to sit on.

Two-burner stove. You can spend as much as you want on a camp stove, but the classic Coleman two-burner stove costs around fifty dollars and will provide years of solid performance.

Dutch oven. Camp cooking with a Dutch oven is an art form (entire cookbooks have been devoted to it), but trust me, even a half-bad Dutch oven chocolate cake will blow the minds of your entire camping party.

Lanterns. A headlamp will take care of your basic illumination needs, but a lantern or two on a picnic table can create a warm ambience. Which is not as great as Dutch oven chocolate cake, but is pretty nice.

Popular Destinations

Moab (Utah). The adventure capital of the Desert Southwest, Moab is home to dozens of commercial and public-lands campgrounds containing hundreds of campsites. It's popular during all but the coldest months of the year.

Yosemite National Park (California). The massive granite domes, monoliths, and peaks of Yosemite have captivated visitors since before John Muir wrote about them in the mid-1800s and made the Sierra Nevada famous. Summer in Yosemite is a busy time, for good reason.

Yellowstone National Park (Wyoming, Montana, and Idaho). America's first national park, Yellowstone is a summer vacation staple for families from all over the country who flock to see bison, elk, geothermal features, and the occasional bear.

Great Smoky Mountains National Park (Tennessee and North Carolina). The most-visited national park in the United States, the Smokies draw families from all over the country to ten campgrounds throughout the park.

Icefields Parkway (Alberta, Canada). The highway connecting Banff and Jasper National Parks is one of the most scenic drives in North America, and the corridor is home to more than a dozen campgrounds. Just make sure you plan well in advance and make reservations—the camping here is no secret (for understandable reasons).

Any state or county park with campsites. You're one Internet search away from finding something nearby. The locale may not be famous, but it will make your week.

Set Up a Tent

If this is your first go-around with a tent or you are borrowing one from a friend, it's a good idea to set it up in your yard or in a nearby park *before* your camping trip—at the very least to make sure no parts are missing. Every tent is different, from cavernous ten-person family tents with multiple rooms to one-person ultralight backpacking tents, but they mostly operate with the same parts and on the same structural principles.

The setup should follow a few basic steps. (1) First, remove the tent from its stuff sack and locate all the parts: poles, stakes, tent body, and rain fly (group together the parts that come in multiples). (2) Then lay out the tent body. Make sure one end isn't pointing downhill, that the doors won't be opening directly into a bush or tree, and that you're not setting the tent on top of sharp sticks or rocks. Weigh the tent down with a rock or something else sturdy while you do the next step: setting up the poles.

(3) Contemporary tent poles are made of aluminum or another lightweight material and will be connected by an internal bungee cord—that is, they sort of assemble themselves with a little direction from you. Just make sure the sections fit together snugly, or you might snap off a pole end once you add tension to the poles (and that's not a good thing, or an easy repair). Once the poles are assembled, slide them into the corresponding fabric sleeves or plastic clips on the tent, and through the grommets at the tie-downs at the bottom of the tent. (4) Then attach the rain fly via clips or hooks, (5) and stake the tent down, starting with the tie-downs on the body, then the doors, then any additional guylines. Make sure everything is as taut as possible . . . unless you want to sleep with the sound of wind flapping your tent fabric all night.

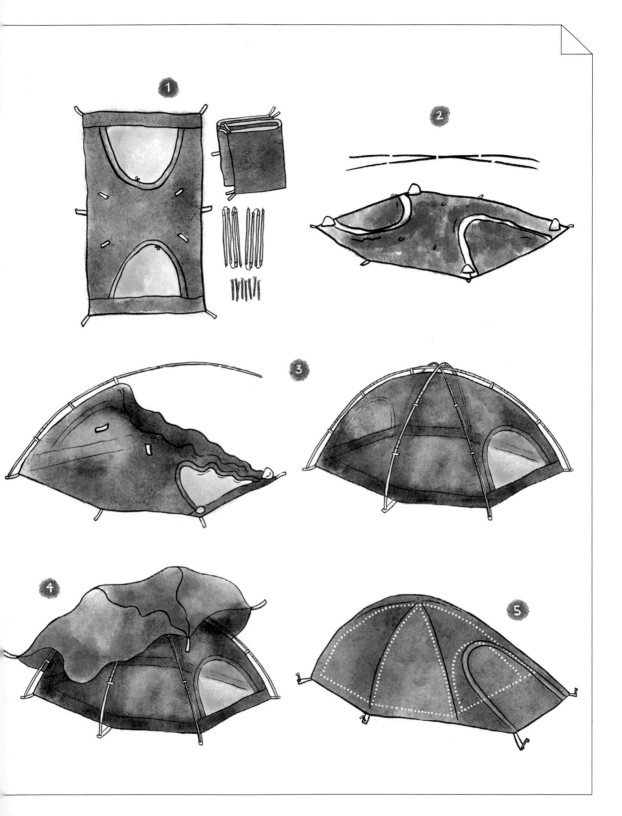

"THE LOVE OF WILDERNESS IS MORE
THAN A HUNGER FOR WHAT IS
ALWAYS BEYOND REACH; IT IS ALSO
AN EXPRESSION OF LOYALTY TO THE
EARTH, THE EARTH WHICH BORE US AND
SUSTAINS US, THE ONLY PARADISE WE
SHALL EVER KNOW, THE ONLY PARADISE
WE EVER NEED, IF ONLY WE HAD
THE EYES TO SEE."

—EDWARD ABBEY,
DOWN THE RIVER

Right: A camper shakes their tent to clean out debris before packing it up in the morning. **Below:** A camper rolls up their sleeping pad and removes gear from the tent.

Left: A small, packable cook set can work for backpacking as well as car camping. **Below:** A small hatchet is indispensable for chopping wood into manageable chunks to use in a campfire. **Bottom:** Cards clipped to a campsite post show that it's been reserved for the weekend.

TEN TIPS FOR CAMPING WITH KIDS

Camping adventures with your children can make for some of the longest-lasting family lore and gives your kids a million memories of growing up. A few easy steps can make it a positive experience for everyone.

1) Do a test run beforehand, if you can. Camping in the backyard is a much lower-stakes affair and will help you determine if your kids (and you) are ready for a full-on camping excursion.

2) Let each of your kids pack a bag with his or her stuff, so you're not spending the entire trip looking for their things in a big bag of communal gear. (Check their packing job to make sure they have included the important items they'll need.)

3) Bring the kids' bikes, if you can. When you want to relax, they can explore the campground.

4) Pack some familiar toys or games so the transition to a new place isn't a completely jarring experience. Consider leaving electronic devices at home, unless you're prepared to recharge and keep track of them.

5) Involve the kids in camp life. Have them get water and collect firewood, and let them help set up camp (roll out sleeping bags, etc.).

6) Make sure you've packed enough warm layers for everyone.

7) Bring an extra tent that your kids can play in (a godsend if it rains).

8) Bring hand sanitizer and make sure everyone uses it—norovirus isn't fun, and it's even less fun when the whole family becomes infected.

9) Bring earplugs. For yourself.

10) Don't forget: flashlights and/or headlamps (and batteries), insect repellent, firewood, a lighter, and supplies for s'mores.

Cooking While Camping

Overnight camping may be considered roughing it but you shouldn't have to rough it when it comes to food. With a little thoughtful planning and the recognition that there are no rules for cooking while camping, you can return from your camping excursion wishing you ate as well every night.

For example, no one is stopping you from grabbing a pizza or Thai takeout on your way out of town and eating that for your first dinner around the campsite fire. You don't have to subsist entirely on freeze-dried backpacking meals sold in an outdoor store, yet if you choose to serve one, you can spice it up by adding fresh vegetables, hot peppers, or cheese to the dried ingredients.

"Hunger is the best seasoning," so any food tastes better when you have an appetite. After a day of hiking and spending time in fresh air, any camp dinner can take on a three-Michelin-star-esque flavor. Here are tips for making the most of your camp cooking situation.

Car Camping

• If you can cook a meal in one pot or pan on your stove at home, you can do the same when you're camping.

• To keep cold items cold, use one or two frozen-solid one-gallon jugs of water in your cooler instead of loose ice.

• Keep your cooler closed during your trip; the food will remain colder. Keep the cooler out of direct sunlight, too.

- Set a large bottle of hand sanitizer on the picnic table as a reminder to everyone to clean their hands and prevent unpleasant germs from spreading.

Backcountry Camping

- If you must have your morning caffeine fix, microground coffee packets like Starbucks Via and Alpine Start make great-tasting java, are easy to carry, and leave zero mess afterward, which is ideal for backcountry trips.

- Chocolate bars will melt, but made-ahead brownies and cookies are portable and will taste yummy even if they get crushed.

- Lots of cheeses can handle a day or five without refrigeration. Generally the harder a cheese, the longer it will be okay to eat in the backcountry.

- Never underestimate the morale boost that a small bottle of hot sauce can provide. The same goes for other spices and seasonings. Carry a stash of salt, ground black pepper, ground ginger, chili powder, ground cumin, cardamom, and red pepper flakes to amp up the flavor in whatever you cook.

- Beware of the astronomical fiber content of some freeze-dried meals (check the nutrition facts label before buying). Some recipes are tasty but can lead to uncomfortable nights in a tent.

- Hot after-dinner beverages, such as lemon-ginger tea and hot chocolate, are great around the campfire and will help you stay hydrated through the night.

- Bring a few small plastic bags for trash. Double-bag them if you're dumping in wet coffee grounds or food scraps.

- It's difficult to get dishes 100 percent clean in the backcountry. Carrying a small pot scraper with you can do wonders toward removing cooked-on crud.

Camping—or full-time living—out of vans has been going on for a while, long before William Least Heat-Moon's *Blue Highways* was published in the 1980s, before Chris Farley played a motivational speaker who "lived in a van down by the river" on *Saturday Night Live* in the 1990s, long before Foster Huntington created the viral hashtag #vanlife in the 2010s.

A van camper wakes up after a night sleeping on a plush mattress in the back of their van.

But van life hasn't been *cool* for that long. In the mid-2010s, the imagery of van life exploded, thanks to the aesthetic and idyllic photos of VW buses and other vehicles piloted by young nomads willing to share scenes from their lives on the road on Instagram.

Imagery and the zeitgeist aside, van life, whether it's for a weekend or a year, can be fun. It's popular for a handful of reasons: You don't necessarily need to park in a campground (in many areas in the western United States, at least). You can pack a lot of stuff in a van (including a real bed mattress). And compared to car camping, van life can be quite cushy (if a little cramped). Van camping is like traveling in an RV without the hassle of driving a large vehicle and without a chemical toilet inside (but also without an RV's interior space).

Vans have been popular with rock climbers for decades because of these reasons and more: the ability to easily relocate "camp" when you want to move on to the next climbing area, their suitability as a rent-free residence while living cheaply to focus on climbing, and their modest size, making possible the occasional night stealthily sleeping in a big-box store parking lot (be sure you learn which stores allow overnight parking).

Vans outfitted for van camping or van life range from old domestic vans with basic bed and storage setups (mattress on the floor, gear in plastic bins) to rebuilt classic Volkswagen vans to six-figure converted Sprinter-style vans with custom wood cabinetry.

It's hard to argue with a rented camper van as the best way to road trip through a new state or country. Fly somewhere, pick up your camper van, throw your bags in the back, get some groceries, and you're off to ramble to your heart's content. As long as you can find a legal place to park overnight, the world is your oyster—moving on to a new place each day, no hauling your luggage in and out of hotel rooms or Airbnb units every night, only stopping for groceries, gas, and the occasional shower.

Gear

Van. Of course, the van is the biggest piece of gear required for van camping. Any van that runs reliably will do, but all-wheel-drive or four-wheel-drive can be desirable if you're taking it into snowy terrain. You can spend a couple thousand dollars on an old van and fix it up yourself, or more than a hundred thousand on a custom-designed, fully kitted-out van. If you want to try before you buy, rental companies like Jucy and Escape Campervans rent out vans in various sizes and capacities.

Mattress. Sleeping on an actual mattress might be one of the best things about van camping. Most folks who build out a van will grab a low-profile (but comfy) mattress from a furniture store, but your only limits are how much storage/living space you want to sacrifice for your sleeping area and how much sleeping room you think you need. And, of course, the dimensions of your van—if you can't possibly get a good night's sleep on anything other than a California king mattress, well, van life may not be for you.

Platform. A bed platform, expertly designed and built, or solidly built by an amateur carpenter, will create tons of storage space in your van. If you simply toss a mattress on the floor and put all your gear/food/luggage around or on top of it, you'll have to reckon with all that stuff when it's time to sleep. The area under your bed is the best place to store your belongings.

Cooler. Even if you don't always (or ever) keep ice in it, a cooler can serve as a place to preserve food (if the cooler gets cold at night, it will retain some chill during the day and at least keep your spinach fresh for more than a few hours inside a hot van) or as a dedicated pantry (keeping your food separate from, you know, critters or dirty laundry).

Top: Finding a free, legal van camping spot is easy in the public lands of the American West. **Far Right:** A small drawer holds all the flatware and cooking supplies needed in a van built for two. **Right:** A rack holds some of the hygienic luxuries of van camping: dish soap, hand sanitizer, and even an electric toothbrush.

Popular Destinations

American West. The western United States is a magnet for van camping because of the sheer size of its public landmass. Some (but not all) US Forest Service and Bureau of Land Management land allows dispersed camping, meaning if you can find a semiprivate place to pull off the road, you can stay there for the night. The desert Southwest in particular is a great location for van camping; its dry, warm climate often translates to more of your time spent sightseeing and less time waiting out rainstorms and/or being stuck in the mud. Plus the temperatures are warm enough for hiking, sightseeing, and van camping for almost the entire spring and fall (and even early and late summer, depending on your heat tolerance).

New Zealand. If you think van camping is popular in the United States, after a few hours driving around New Zealand's most scenic areas, you'll wonder if every tenth vehicle in the country is a rented camper van. Several rental companies (with shuttles from airports) make it easy for shorter visits, and a healthy market of camper van buyers and sellers may tempt you into longer stays.

Canada. Most of British Columbia's recreational sites offer free camping or camping for a small fee, and in other Canadian provinces, free camping is available on many locations on Canada's crown land (land owned by the government).

Build a Basic Bed Platform

One of the biggest pluses of van camping is the cushy bed. You could toss a mattress in the back of your van and call it good, but you'll soon find yourself constantly relocating piles of stuff so you can sleep or move around the back of the van. Solution: Elevate the bed, just a bit, to create storage space underneath it. You don't have to get fancy (although you can if you wish)— you're just building a sturdy table.

One of the simplest ways to elevate the sleeping area is to take an accurate measurement of the length and width of your bed platform and have a large four- by eight-foot sheet of plywood cut to those dimensions (home improvement stores will usually do two cuts for free). (1) Next, build a basic frame out of two-by-fours on the bottom of the plywood, along the outside edges, with a strip of lumber lengthwise down the center to support the middle of the bed. (2) Build a second frame in this same shape (this will be the base of your bed frame), then join the two frames with two-by-four supports of the appropriate height (twelve to eighteen inches) for your van. (3) Finally, attach your plywood sheet to the top of the frame and toss your mattress on top. Remember: You want to maximize your storage space, but you also want to be able to sit up in bed and not hit your head on the ceiling once the mattress is positioned on top of the platform.

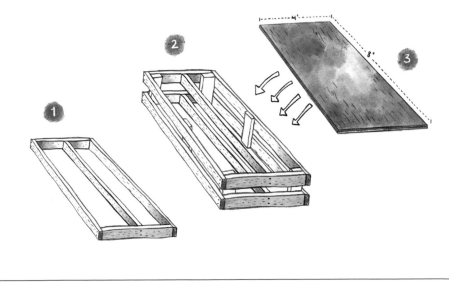

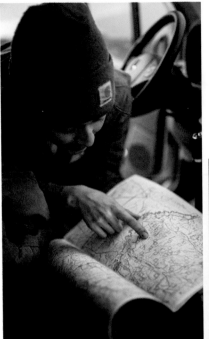

Left: A van camper examines an atlas to find the next campsite. **Below:** A trip journal with instant photos. **Bottom:** A morning pour-over makes van camping feel like home.

"TO THOSE DEVOID OF IMAGINATION
A BLANK PLACE ON THE MAP
IS A USELESS WASTE; TO OTHERS,
THE MOST VALUABLE PART."

—ALDO LEOPOLD,
*A SAND COUNTY ALMANAC:
AND SKETCHES HERE AND THERE*

How to Spend a Month Camping without Quitting Your Job

If we go camping a couple weekends a year, we think, *Hey, that's a pretty good year*. And it is. But if a couple weekends a year is pretty good, a whole month of camping must be better than pretty good, right? Pretty great? Fantastic? Amazing?

If you camp a month's worth of nights in one year, it will indeed be better than pretty good. It will be fantastic. (I'll also tell you that two weeks' worth of nights outside is phenomenal, in case you have so much going on that a month is impossible. But hear me out before you decide that.) Sleeping outside in a sleeping bag—away from household chores and tasks, e-mail, 4G/LTE data, and all the busyness that melts away when you're a few miles from a paved road—is a night that feels like a memory being made instead of another turn of the gears of a routine life.

So how do you achieve it? Motivation, math, and a little planning.

Motivation first: You have to want to do it. Then you must commit to it. Like anything else in life, finding the motivation can be challenging but worth it in the end. You have to tell yourself you're going to do it. *I am going to spend a month outside this year.*

Next, the math: Let's say, for example, your job allows you two weeks of vacation. That's fourteen days. If you take one chunk of five consecutive days at one time, bookended with a weekend on either side, that's nine days total. If you left on a Friday and camped every night of that stint, you'd sleep outside for nine straight nights, then head home on a Sunday to unpack, do laundry, and sleep in your own bed before heading to work on

Monday. Do that twice, and that's eighteen days of camping—and you still have four vacation days remaining.

If you consider your two weeks of vacation and the weekends of summer, here's how many days you won't be at work, assuming you work five days a week, Monday through Friday:

Vacation: 14 days
Memorial Day weekend: 3 days
Weekends between Memorial Day and Labor Day (17): 34 days
Labor Day weekend: 3 days
TOTAL: 54 days

Yes, you'd like to spend a few days and nights of your summer at music festivals, sleeping in and going to brunch, lying around in the park, barbecuing, and going to ball games. That's reasonable. But even if you blow twenty-three of those vacation/weekend days doing the brunch/ball/barbecue/sleeping-in things, you still have thirty-one days left over to go camping. Seems like a lot when you actually do the math, eh? So it should be pretty easy to camp for a month . . . right? Math is a magical thing.

That brings us to the third point: planning. If you plan, making time for camping will be easier. Begin by knowing where all your camping equipment is stored and pulling your gear and supplies together early in the year so you can bolt out the door at a moment's notice. When you have your stuff at the ready, you can drive out of town Friday immediately after work and land at the campground or campsite Friday evening. Otherwise, you may find yourself digging through a closet, garage, or storage unit at eight on a Saturday morning and realizing you need to buy stove fuel—or a stove.

A month is a lot of nights under the stars, of course. But if camping is something that brings you joy, then more camping would equal more joy, wouldn't it? Seems worth trying, anyway.

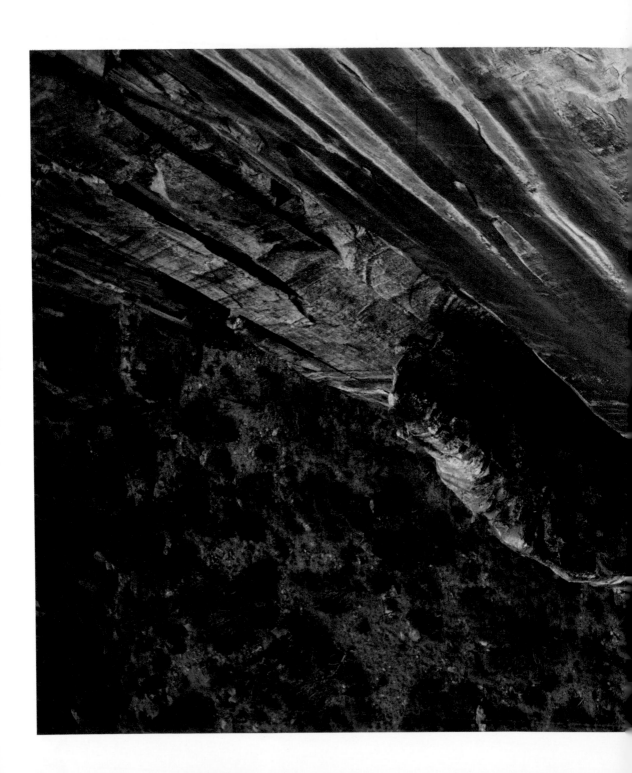

The most extreme kind of camping happens a thousand or more feet off the ground, tethered to a rock wall, with nothing more underneath you than a thin layer of fabric supported by aluminum tubing. This kind of camping is nirvana to big wall rock climbers—it's where their days end and begin on multiday climbing routes.

Camping hundreds of feet off the ground isn't the easiest concept to wrap your head around. Most people's first question is "Why?" followed by "How?" The why is fairly simple to answer: The rock climbs on formations like Yosemite's El Capitan and the sandstone walls of Zion National Park are so long and difficult that they can't easily be completed in a single day. Instead of rappelling back down to the bottom every day, climbers just sleep up on the wall. This may not sound like a reasonable hobby, and that's not incorrect. But that's the functional answer to why climbers sleep up high on big wall climbs. The existential answer is more complicated and difficult to formulate.

So how do you do it? In the early days of pioneering big wall climbs, climbers slept in hammocks suspended from the granite face of El Capitan. We've come a long ways from hammocks. Nowadays, climbers sleep on portaledges, which are essentially cots, but instead of standing on legs, they're suspended from above. Portaledges are either single or double; that is, wide enough for one person or two people. They're secured to the rock with bolts or other climbing protection devices, and climbers are always secured to the rock via ropes and their harnesses—even while sleeping and going number one and number two.

Everything needed for the climb, and camping, is pulled up in haul bags—large, extremely durable duffels that hold portaledges, sleeping bags, cooking gear, climbing gear, food, extra clothes, and water (there are no sources of water on big wall climbs, so climbers must bring all their water with them, usually one gallon per person per day of climbing). With two or three climbers, and climbs sometimes lasting up to a week or more, and a gallon of water weighing eight pounds, you can imagine how heavy haul bags get. Every time the team completes a climbing pitch (roughly seventy-five to two hundred feet long), all the bags have to be hauled up manually. Obviously, there are no restrooms on big walls, so climbers go in bags, and the bags are stuffed into a PVC "poop tube" or a separate haul bag that seals in the smell of the human waste inside (just kidding, it totally smells like poop).

Perhaps the most intricate part of the big wall camping setup is the system of ropes involved in keeping the climbers and their stuff safely secured to the wall: Look at a simple setup for two climbers camping for just one night, and all the ropes and carabiners can look like a very complicated mess. But the climbers have a solid idea of what's tied to what, and everyone is hyperconscious of the big expanse of open air all around and below the "camp."

Not surprisingly, few people climb simply to camp on a big wall, because this is more labor intensive than probably any other type of camping, with all the hauling of gear, improvising rope systems, and assembling portaledges in midair as the sun sets. This type of camping is more a result of wanting to climb big, sheer rock faces. It's also one of the most high-consequence camping scenarios: If you drop your phone while taking a photo of your backpacking campsite, it might crack the screen or get a little dirty. If you drop your phone while taking a photo of your big wall campsite, you'll likely never see your phone again, and if you do, it will be in more than one piece. Same thing with your toothbrush, your spork, and so on.

Despite the exposure, the hard work, and the consequences, many climbers will tell you that they sleep better on portaledges on big wall climbs than they sleep at home. You're a long way from e-mail, to-do lists, and yardwork up there on the cliff, that's for sure, and the singularity of the situation makes it easy to stay in the moment. Even if you don't sleep well, it's tough to spend a night on a big wall and not come away with an incredible memory.

Popular Destinations

There are long climbs all over the American West but only a couple big wall destinations—places where rock climbs are steep and of sustained difficulty that require spending the night on a portaledge anchored to the rock (as opposed to a rock ledge, which is more common on alpine/mountain climbs). Yosemite National Park (specifically its three-thousand-foot monolith El Capitan) and Zion National Park are the two most common places you'll see big wall camping in the United States.

A single portaledge hangs
hundreds of feet off the
ground, beneath climbing
gear and a haul bag.

Big wall camping requires
multiple ropes for climbing,
hauling, and securing gear
on the wall.

Gear

Portaledge. A portaledge is made with an aluminum frame and a fabric floor, and its tubing comes apart in sections for packing and transport. Climbers haul portaledges up the wall and assemble them nightly. (The tubing is connected by cord, so you can't drop a piece of tubing into the abyss during setup.)

Haul bags (aka pigs). These are made of durable vinyl-coated material that can withstand being dragged up rock walls for hundreds of feet. You'd never drag an unprotected tent or sleeping bag up a wall because it would be totally shredded after a few dozen feet—so you put it in a haul bag for protection.

Poop tubes. In the old days, when fewer climbers were camping on big walls, they used to just do their business into the air and let gravity take care of it. You can imagine how this stopped working so well once there were more climbers camping out on a mountain. So human waste goes into plastic bags, and the plastic bags go up the wall with climbers, in PVC tubes with caps on both ends or dedicated haul bags.

Hanging stove. Camping a few hundred feet off the ground means there's nothing to set your stove on, so wall campers invest in a hanging stove, a canister-style stove with a suspension system that enables it to hang in the air while you cook.

Ascenders (aka *jumars*). Ascenders are handheld devices that allow climbers to pull themselves up ropes that are anchored from above—essentially a handle that grips the rope so it can slide up, but not down. In big wall climbing, ascenders are also used to pull haul bags up the wall. A climber attaches the ascender to the rope tied to a haul bag, and attaches a loop of webbing to the ascender and stands on it to weight it, pulling a few feet of rope up at a time until the bag reaches the climber.

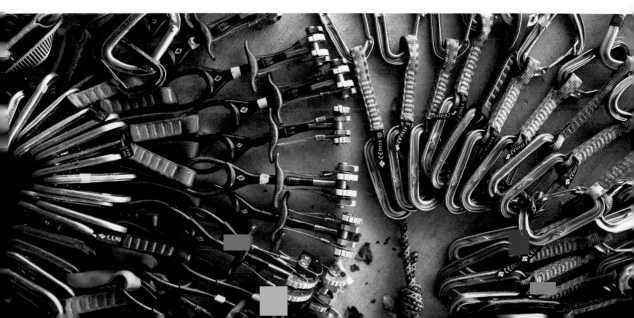

Above: A pair of aiders, webbed ladders used for ascending a route, hang on a wall. **Above Right:** A climber works to assemble a portaledge high above the ground on a climb. **Right:** When you're hundreds of feet off the ground everything needs to be affixed, so water bottles, a coffee mug, and belay gloves are clipped to a strap.

Below Left: A "poop tube" sits off to the side in a small alcove of rock on the route. **Below Right:** A climber stops to look up at a route while carrying gear to the base of the wall.

Haul a Pig/Haul Bag up a Big Wall

When you're climbing and camping on a big wall, all your gear comes with you—which means you have to physically pull it up the wall alongside your climbing route. Thankfully, a few pieces of technology provide mechanical advantages to make it a little easier than just hand-over-hand pulling. Once at the top of a pitch, you'll clip the end of the rope attached to the pig (or haul bag) to your anchor, then clip a progress capture device (such as a Petzl Mini Traxion) to the anchor. Pull up the slack in the rope and thread it through the progress capture device so that the teeth keep the unweighted end of the rope (the one you clipped to the anchor) from slipping through the device. Next, take your ascender and clip it to your belay loop via a daisy chain, then clip the ascender to the unweighted end of the rope. You're now ready to haul the bag—take the slack out of the system and once the rope goes taut, you'll haul the bag up in small increments by sliding the ascender all the way up the anchor, then sitting down to weight the ascender and pull the rope through the system and begin raising the haul bag, repeating this process several dozen times to get the bag to your position.

At first it feels like the bag isn't moving at all. This is because it isn't; you're getting all the slack out of the system. Once that happens, the bag will begin to shift slowly upward. Several minutes later, if you don't hit any snags, the bag will be at the anchor, and you'll clip it into the anchor and remove the haul line from your system.

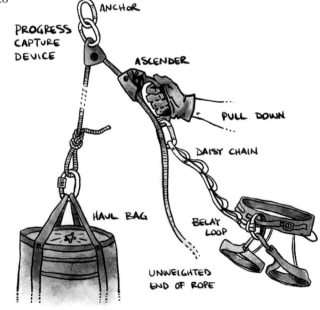

ANCHOR

PROGRESS
CAPTURE
DEVICE

ASCENDER

PULL DOWN

DAISY CHAIN

HAUL BAG

BELAY
LOOP

UNWEIGHTED
END OF ROPE

"ONE OF THE UNDERAPPRECIATED BENEFITS OF VENTURING INTO REMOTE LANDSCAPES IS THAT WE ARE OFTEN THROWN INTO CONNECTING WITH EACH OTHER."

—FLORENCE WILLIAMS, *THE NATURE FIX: WHY NATURE MAKES US HAPPIER, HEALTHIER, AND MORE CREATIVE*

How's this sound for a vacation? Every day, you pop yourself into a small boat, paddle across calm waters for a couple hours, stop for lunch, paddle for a couple more hours, then call it a day. Every night, you sleep somewhere different, under the stars and next to the water. Every morning, you set off for a new destination.

That's essentially kayak touring. It's like backpacking in that you're using your own power to get from place to place, but you're not carrying a thirty- to forty-pound load on your back and walking up and down trails. You're gliding over the water, propelling yourself with your paddle strokes, moving quickly enough to get somewhere new but slowly enough to notice everything.

Unlike other self-propelled styles of camping (like backpacking and bikepacking), what you pack in a kayak is limited more by volume than by weight, since you're not carrying your gear and food on your person. So as long as space allows, you can bring whatever you want—within reason. Obviously, if you fill up a rear hatch with cans of your favorite IPA, your kayak will be a little challenging to steer, and if you fill the whole kayak with heavy things (like beer), it may sink below the waterline when you step in it. So maybe leave the kettlebells at home, too.

Once you've figured out how to pack and fit your belongings into a kayak, this type of camping is just like any other type of camping, only you paddle between campsites. Depending on where you go, overnight or multiday kayak tours can take you from island to island (like in Washington's San Juan Islands), circumnavigating a big body of water (like Lake Tahoe), or down a mellow river. Kayak touring can even be a bit like a beach vacation, but one geared for people who want to spend their days paddling to the next beach instead of relaxing on the sand all day.

THE CAMPING LIFE

Gear

Touring kayak. This long, stable kayak has multiple hatches for storing overnight gear and food. The kayak is the most expensive item needed for a kayak tour. You can rent one in many kayaking destinations.

Dry bags. Roll-top, watertight bags made of polyurethane-coated fabric will keep your gear dry in case you flip your boat or your kayak lets a bit of water into the hatches.

Water shoes/sandals. Your feet will get wet no matter what shoes you wear while kayaking, so your shoes might as well let water drain through them. Strappy sandals like those made by Chaco and Teva have been favorites for many years, but more substantial water shoes with improved toe protection are gaining popularity.

PFD. A personal floatation device, aka life jacket, is mandatory in any situation where you may fall into the water.

Paddling gloves. Even if you have tough hands, a pair of paddling gloves can be nice when touring—both to keep the front of your hands from getting beat up from all the paddling and to keep the back of your hands from getting sunburned by sunlight bouncing off the water.

Popular Destinations

San Juan Islands (Washington). This might be the most well-known kayak-touring spot in the western United States, thanks to its calm water, breathtaking scenery, and opportunities to spot whales.

Little Tybee Island (Georgia). An untouched barrier island only reachable by boat, Little Tybee's channels change with the tides and are best navigated by hiring a local guide (Savannah Canoe and Kayak offers overnight and three-day trips).

Prince William Sound (Alaska). Various guided trips on the Prince William Sound tour big scenery (huge granite walls and calving glaciers) and big marine life (humpback and orca whales).

Maine Island Trail (New Hampshire to Canada). This is America's first recreational water trail, connecting more than 200 coastal islands in 375 miles. You don't have to attempt the whole trail at once—many multiday trip options exist.

Baja California (Mexico). Baja's incredible diversity of sea life has earned it the nickname "the Mexican Galápagos," and kayak tours can include sightings of whales, sea turtles, dolphins, and several varieties of tropical birds.

Lake Superior State Water Trail (Wisconsin/Minnesota). This trail connects hundreds of miles of shoreline on a lake that's both big water and has big ships—a guide and/or training is recommended.

Top: A kayaker warms their feet in a small campfire at the end of a day of paddling during a winter trip. **Above Left:** A dromedary bag holds several liters of filtered water in a flexible, durable package. **Above Right:** A camper fills a cooking pot with water filtered from a gravity filter hung on a stand made of kayak paddles.

"WE NEED THE TONIC OF WILDNESS.
. . . AT THE SAME TIME THAT WE ARE
EARNEST TO EXPLORE AND LEARN ALL
THINGS, WE REQUIRE THAT ALL THINGS
BE MYSTERIOUS AND UNEXPLORABLE,
THAT LAND AND SEA BE INDEFINITELY
WILD, UNSURVEYED AND UNFATHOMED
BY US BECAUSE UNFATHOMABLE. WE
CAN NEVER HAVE ENOUGH OF NATURE."

—HENRY DAVID THOREAU, *WALDEN*

Pack a Touring Kayak

When you initially view the amount of space inside a touring kayak's hatches, you might assume you have all the room in the world for your food and camping gear. This is only partly true. The hatches have limitations with their round openings and triangle-shaped compartments. So you'll need a packing strategy. First and foremost, place anything you don't want to get wet, or even damp, in a dry bag. Theoretically the hatches are waterproof, but sometimes they let in a bit of water. That moisture will ruin something like a camera if it's not packed in a dry bag. So, to be safe, put everything you bring in a dry bag. Second, since the kayak hatches aren't always easy to load because of their funny shapes, it's better to divide your provisions and belongings into a half dozen or so dry bags of various sizes rather than three large bags. A giant bag may not fit into a small hatch. Purchase different colors of bags to help you remember what item is in each bag. Then it can be a game of Tetris to stow these modules in the hatches in the right place and order. For example, you can shove your sleeping bag and tent all the way in the front or back of the boat, because you won't need access to them until the end of the day when you set up camp. Other items that you'll want close at hand while paddling—camera, water bottle, snacks, sunscreen, and rain jacket—go into a small dry bag clipped inside your cockpit.

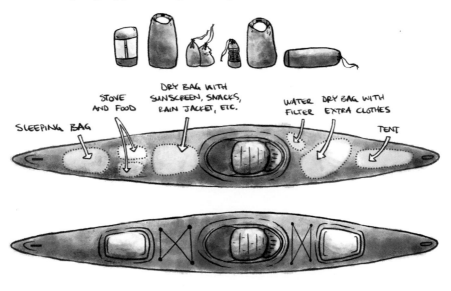

Right: A dinner with fresh vegetables is easy to prepare campside; it's made better with some grains and olive oil. **Below:** A kayaking guide uses a GPS to check the navigation plan for the next day.

Opposite Page; Top Left: Gear can be lashed to the top of a boat for a short portage. **Top Right:** A camper prepares morning coffee, wearing convertible gloves for protection from mosquitoes and no-see-ums. **Bottom:** A group of kayakers makes the most of the last bits of daylight and a small driftwood fire at their lakefront campsite.

A Brief List of Feelings You Can Experience Camping That You (Nearly) Can't Get Anywhere Else

- The satisfaction of finding the perfect log or rock to sit on, even if it's not as comfortable as a chair

- Gratitude for the technology in a waterproof tent fly as raindrops tap (or downpour) on it

- Being present enough to stare into a campfire for several minutes and not get bored doing it

- Being dirty but not feeling dirty because a shower (and society) is several miles away

- The solitude of knowing there are no other human beings within a half-day walk of where you are

- The subconscious calm of having no cell phone service for a couple consecutive days

- The joy of escaping the buzz of overheard cell phone calls, video streaming, or music booming from another person's phone speakers

- The liberation from needing to make choices on food, drink, or reading materials because you're carrying your only options in your pack

- The joy of letting yourself sit next to a lake and stare at it because you have time

- The unexpected increase in joy of eating food after working up a hunger from being outside all day

- The satisfaction of being able to carry everything you need in a pack or the trunk of a car

- Getting lost in conversation with your friends without the distraction of cell phones

- The smell of campfire on your clothes

- Excusing yourself from your household to-do list because you're miles away from laundry, paying bills, repairs, and errands

- Going to bed early when you're tired without any late-night screen time or e-mails to keep you up

- The uninhibited sounds of wild animals

- The rustle of wind moving through the trees

- The view over the top of your morning cup of coffee

- The feeling of not caring what time it is because you only have to worry about when it gets light outside and when it gets dark

- Quenching your thirst with water that's cold because it was snow a few minutes earlier

Imagine backpacking, either in the hiking-on-trails sense or the traipsing-around-Europe-during-a-gap-year sense, carrying everything you need with you, going slow enough to take in the world around you. Imagine, in addition, that you don't have to carry everything on your back. And that you can coast.

Bike touring, or bikepacking, as it's increasingly been called over the past decade, is one of the most fun human-powered methods of traveling. Yes, you have to pedal up hills, but once you're at the top, you can coast down the other side. And the weight of your gear is never crushing your shoulders and hips—it's strapped to your bicycle.

Traditionally, bicycle tourists kept to paved roads, but improvements in off-road bikes and specially made bags for off-road bikes have helped foster a surge in dirt road and trail bikepacking. Both on-road and off-road riding are fun ways to travel—you're not speeding by scenery in a car, but you're not walking at a slow pace either.

When you tour on roads, you can alternate nights of camping with nights at hotels or bed-and-breakfasts, creating a semi–"roughing it" tour. When you choose dirt roads or trails, you'll probably do a lot more camping. Either way, any time you want to stop for a snack or a rest, you simply lean your bike up against a tree, a roadside café, or convenience store.

If you're touring on roads or stopping in towns along your route, you might discover that a fully loaded touring bicycle is a disarming accessory. Total strangers will feel comfortable walking up to you and asking about where you're headed, how far you ride every day, where you sleep, and how much you eat.

It's helpful, but not necessary, to have camping experience before you head out on a bike tour. Aside from the bicycling gear, however, no specialized camping gear is needed. Anything you use for backpacking will work on a bike tour, including but not limited to backpacking tents, sleeping bags and sleeping pads, stoves, and cookware.

Any road or trail (outside of designated wilderness) is a bike-tourable route, as long as you are comfortable with the terrain and traffic. That said, lots of trails would be miserable if undertaken on a bicycle, so start your search with trails known for mountain biking, or with jeep roads. In the United States, the Adventure Cycling Association works to establish quality, safe bike-touring routes all over the country, and it publishes the routes on its website at adventurecycling.org.

THE CAMPING LIFE

Popular Destinations

C&O Canal Towpath. This 184.5-mile-long towpath, originally built in the mid-1800s for mules to tow boats on the Chesapeake and Ohio Canal between Washington, DC, and Cumberland, Maryland, became a national historic park in 1971 and has been a favorite of cyclists ever since. The path isn't paved—it's a crushed-rock and clay surface—but it's almost completely flat, and there are campsites approximately every five miles along the way. Touring cyclists can do trips of varying lengths on the towpath, from quick overnights to traverses of the entire trail.

TransAmerica Trail. Originally developed for Bikecentennial '76 to celebrate America's two hundredth anniversary in 1976, the TransAm is probably the United States's most famous cross-country road-cycling route, covering 4,223 miles from Astoria, Oregon, to Yorktown, Virginia, and passing through Yellowstone and Grand Teton National Parks on its way through ten states.

Great Divide Mountain Bike Route. One of the most famous bike routes designed by the Adventure Cycling Association, this route parallels the Continental Divide, starting in Jasper, Alberta, ending in Antelope Wells, New Mexico, and covering 3,083 miles on mostly dirt roads with a small amount of single track. The route runs through several towns, allowing ample opportunities to shower and resupply.

White Rim Trail. A one hundred–mile mountain bike ride on jeep roads through the slickrock desert in Canyonlands National Park near Moab in Utah, this popular tour is usually split up over three or four days, with cyclists spending nights at established campsites along the White Rim, a band of cliffs a thousand feet above the Colorado and Green Rivers. Most cyclists do this route with vehicle support—that is, a friend drives a high-clearance, four-wheel-drive vehicle with all the camping gear, food, and water behind the cyclists, who only carry what they need to ride twenty-five to thirty-five miles each day.

Pacific Coast Route. A route from Vancouver, British Columbia, to San Diego, California, the 1,848-mile Pacific Coast Route puts the ocean at your left, or your right, for almost your entire trip. The route can be done in one monthlong (or two-monthlong) stint of riding forty to sixty miles per day, but it can also conveniently be split into manageable chunks between cities—Vancouver to Portland, Portland to San Francisco, San Francisco to San Diego.

Nordic Countries. Norway, Sweden, and Finland all have some version of *allemansrätten*, or "the right to roam," which means you can camp on any land as long as it's 150 meters from a building (i.e., someone's house). This, and the scenery, make these countries fairly ideal bike-touring destinations—especially Norway's Lofoten Islands.

Gear

Bike bags. Panniers, the saddlebag-type bags you find on road-touring bikes, are usually waterproof and have enough room for almost anything you need to take on a bike tour (within reason). They require special racks on the front and back of a bike but, once secured, are a stable way to carry gear. Frame bags, more commonly used on dirt-road and trail touring and attach directly to the bike frame instead of pannier racks, require more thought when packing, since they're generally less spacious and more odd-shaped. But once you get the hang of packing your stuff in them, you'll be happy to have your gear strapped to your bike and not to your back.

Touring bicycle. For paved-road tours, lots of different bikes will work, depending on how you want to carry your gear. Unlike mountain bikes and road bikes, touring bikes do not need to be especially expensive (or even new) and are still often made of steel, a strong and stiff frame material that's less common in high-end mountain and road bikes built for speed and performance. Select a stable, tough bike. You can be less conscious about bike weight, since you're strapping twenty to thirty pounds of gear and food to it every time you ride. If you want to use panniers, your bike will need braze-ons or mounts for bike racks on the front and back of the bike. If you want to use frame bags, you'll be able to strap them to almost any bike.

Water bottles or hydration backpack. You'll need to hydrate, and the method you use depends on how you rig bags to your bike. If you have panniers, you can use water bottles in cages mounted on your bike frame or a hydration backpack. But if you have frame bags, they might take up the space on the bike frame where water bottles are usually mounted, so you'll have to find another spot for your water bottles or wear a hydration backpack.

Bike helmet. The type of helmet is up to the individual rider, but almost all helmets offer better protection for your brain than your skull alone.

Bike repair kit and extra tubes. The biggest showstopper on a bike tour can be a broken bike part. Thankfully, with a recently tuned-up bike, you shouldn't have any problems. Flat tires, however, can put a hitch in a day of cycling, so if you're going on a bike tour, it's a good idea to get a pair of puncture-resistant tires installed on your bike before you go, and to carry a patch kit, pump, and extra tube (and the know-how to fix a flat tire). A few basic bike repair tools such as a light pedal wrench, a rag and chain cleaner/lube, and a multitool with Allen wrenches, a spoke wrench, a chain tool, and several screwdriver bits can be helpful as well. Even if nothing goes wrong with your bike, it's nice to have a multitool to make small adjustments and tighten bike parts during your ride.

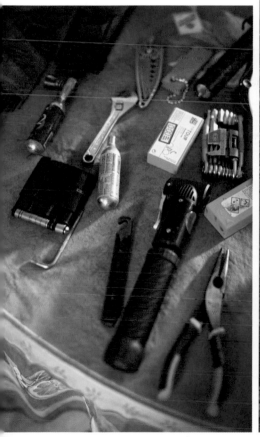

A basic kit of bike tools includes Allen wrenches, CO_2 cartridges, tire levers, a small pump, patch kits, multitools, and needle nose pliers.

A frame bag fits perfectly in the bike's triangle and adds lots of storage to hold touring essentials.

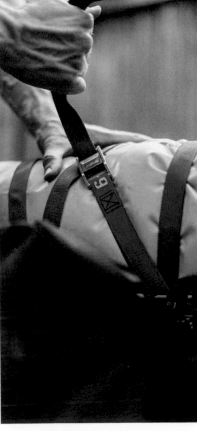

Top: Cyclists pedal fully loaded touring bikes on a car-free trail. **Above:** An assortment of bungee cords is useful for strapping items to bike racks. **Left:** A cyclist tightens a bag of gear onto their bicycle's rear rack with a raft strap.

"IN CHARGING ORDINARY MOVEMENT
WITH MOMENTUM, A BIKE TRIP OFFERS
THAT RAREST, MOST ELUSIVE OF THINGS
IN OUR FRENETIC WORLD: CLARITY OF
PURPOSE. YOUR SOLE RESPONSIBILITY
ON EARTH, AS LONG AS YOUR LEGS
LAST EACH DAY, IS TO BREATHE, PEDAL,
BREATHE—AND LOOK AROUND."

—KATE HARRIS,
*LANDS OF LOST BORDERS:
A JOURNEY ON THE SILK ROAD*

Sleeping in a hut may not be the first image that comes to mind when most of us hear the word *camping*. After all, the inside of a mountain hut is hardly the "outdoors." But most mountain huts bring you close to nature and allow you to rough it to some degree— although the experiences differ all over the world.

In the Appalachian Mountain Club's White Mountain huts in New Hampshire, for example, you'll sleep in a bunk with a pillow and blankets provided, as well as breakfast, lunch, and cold running water. In most of the mountain huts in the Alps in France and Switzerland, the bunk situation is similar, but there's often no running water because of the huts' positions high in the mountains, above reliable streams or creeks. One advantage of hut camping in France and Switzerland is that breakfast and dinner are included, and often there's a small made-to-order menu for lunch, too. The huts in Italy's Dolomites are similar to their French and Swiss cousins, but with more extensive daytime menus, and they're almost always equipped with an espresso machine. The government-run huts in New Zealand are more basic and don't include a kitchen staff or meals, but gas cookers are often provided for guest usage.

Sleeping in most huts is communal and coed, often with six, ten, or twenty-five people in the same room. Families can stay together (or as near to each other as they'd like). The blankets and pillowcases in most mountain huts aren't washed between boarders, so you're required to bring a sleep sack or sleeping bag liner to keep the blankets clean. Sleeping in the same room as a dozen or more strangers has its challenges (bring earplugs), but you remind yourself how much lighter you're traveling during the day without carrying a tent (four to five pounds), sleeping bag (two to three pounds), sleeping pad (one to two pounds), pots and stove (one to two pounds), and the food for all your meals.

The presence of mountain huts in the landscape can appear a bit jarring to an American eye. But huts enable exploration of places like the Alps and the Andes by greater numbers of people and with far less environmental impact. If you spend an evening in a mountain hut in the Alps with fifty or sixty other folks, then try to imagine all their tents spread out in the same area, you can understand the sensibility of building a hut to accommodate trekkers or skiers. If that doesn't convince you, an evening watching the sunset from a hut patio with a cold beer in your hand might do the trick.

Gear

Sleeping bag liner. Required in many huts, and probably preferred by most everyone.

Earplugs. These can be crucial to get a good night of sleep, especially in hut rooms shared with snorers, early-rising climbers, or campers who have packed their stuff in loud, crinkly plastic bags.

Hut shoes. Many huts don't allow you to wear hiking, mountaineering, or ski boots inside the building, and some provide Crocs or similar slipper-type shoes for you to wear while you're inside. If you'd rather not use communal shoes, bring your own.

Alpine Club membership card. In many mountain huts, you'll get a discount on room and board if you're a member of your country's alpine club. The American Alpine Club card works in many European huts, and the discount is definitely worth carrying your card with you as you hike or ski.

Hand sanitizer. It's useful for huts where there is no running water or no access to water at all.

Above: Climbers hike into a hut to spend the night before an early start the next morning. **Left:** Alpine hut sleeping quarters are sparse but comfortable; bringing your own sleeping bag or sleep sack is a must.

Popular Destinations

AMC White Mountain huts (New Hampshire). The Appalachian Mountain Club's hut system consists of eight huts (the High Huts) on popular trails in the White Mountains and are staffed from June to September or October.

DOC huts (New Zealand). New Zealand's Department of Conservation manages more than 950 huts of various shapes and sizes, ranging from serviced huts staffed by wardens, with cooking facilities, mattresses, water supplies, and more, to basic huts with bunks and no amenities.

SAC huts (Switzerland). The Swiss Alpine Club manages more than 150 huts with 9,000-plus bunks throughout the Alps. All huts are open year-round to some degree (sometimes the entire hut is closed in the winter except for a "winter room" for basic shelter), and most have staffed kitchens.

Bariloche huts (Argentina). Bariloche National Park is home to seven mountain huts, all with basic kitchens and bunks, and some with restaurants for visiting trekkers and climbers.

Dolomite huts (Italy). If you love good coffee and good food, the Dolomite Rifugi in northereast Italy will not disappoint. Booking a reservation can be complicated, so it's best to use a reservation service such as Holimites to arrange your booking.

"EXPLORATION IS NOTHING MORE THAN A FORAY INTO THE UNKNOWN, AND A FOUR-YEAR-OLD CHILD, WANDERING ABOUT ALONG IN THE DEPARTMENT STORE, FITS THE DEFINITION AS WELL AS THE SNOW-BLIND MAN WANDERING ACROSS THE KHYBER PASS. THE EXPLORER IS THE PERSON WHO IS LOST."

—TIM CAHILL,
JAGUARS RIPPED MY FLESH

Top: Skis line the front wall of the alpine hut; the easy access means you can be on the mountain in just a few minutes. **Bottom:** A climber plans out a day and a half of snacks and instant coffee for their party.

Top Left: A hut caretaker writes out the weather forecast for climbers and skiers since there's no cell phone reception or Internet at the hut. **Top Right:** Many huts are self-catering, so this guest washes their dishes to clean up from breakfast. **Left:** The loft of the alpine hut is the perfect spot to store gear and hang-dry apparel.

Adventure Is Better Than Instagram

If you've seen a photo from New Zealand's Instagram-famous Roys Peak, with a person standing on the end of a high ridge that drops away above a panorama of peaks surrounding Lake Wanaka, you might be surprised to learn that the person in the image isn't actually standing on the mountain summit. The photo spot, where on any good-weather day you might find a dozen or more people waiting in line for their photo op, is about 750 vertical feet below the peak.

Traditionally, in the 500-plus-year history of mountain climbing, the summit has been the objective. But nowadays, for many of us, the Instagram viewpoint is the new pinnacle. It certainly is on Roys Peak, where the peak's summit (with its great but not quite picture-perfect view) is not even half as popular as the Instagram spot.

There's nothing wrong with setting your destination for somewhere famous or popular. We're all trying to make the most of our time, to get the best bang for our buck, and word of mouth is one way to identify the "best" spots. There can be comfort and camaraderie in hiking to a place where a lot of people are going. And those spots are popular for good reason—they're beautiful. But be aware that most people go for the low-hanging fruit. If your goal is to get away from crowds and have a unique or somewhat solitary experience, then dig a little deeper than the coveted Instagram pic or the top-ten list. Authentic adventure is exploring your own path, not getting in line or following everyone else.

So if you want to do something that feels more adventurous, here's a piece of advice: Don't choose your destinations based on social media. Do some research, maybe even refer to a map or a guidebook. Or if you use Instagram and other apps to identify good photo spots, consider that within a few miles of a megafamous view is at least one scene that's probably just as beautiful—and you'll likely experience it with far fewer people. Walk farther. Drive a bit longer down that dirt road. Scramble up a side canyon. You'll be able to take your time, find a place to sit, and enjoy the view by yourself for as long as you want. That sort of adventure comes with its own rewards.

Careful, though: If you find that perfect place where no one else is going, you might not want to geotag it on Instagram—at least if you want it to stay your secret.

Glamping is a relatively new term in the outdoors world—the *Merriam-Webster* dictionary traces its first use back to 2005 (about a year after Facebook was launched, if you remember that). It's short for "glamorous camping." Which, historically, probably sounded like an oxymoron.

All the comforts of home can be found in this yurt in upstate New York.

If you have a lot of experience camping, *glamorous* may not be one of the words you'd use to describe it. But glamping offers all the great things about camping—campfires, the sounds, smells, and sights you get when you're close to nature—with quite a bit more amenities and comfort. And you're *this close* to nature.

A glamping adventure is camping for outdoorish folks who don't necessarily want to rough it to enjoy nature. Whether it's spending a night in a canvas wall tent, an Airstream trailer, a yurt, or a rustic cabin, glampers get close to nature without being totally immersed. And they often have access to a flushing toilet and a mattress (or even a real bed, with pillows!).

Finding glamping destinations is easy thanks to websites like Glamping Hub, which provide listings and reservations systems similar to those of Airbnb or Vrbo, except the listings are for treehouses, yurts, safari tents, domes, tepees, camper vans, eco-pods, huts, barns, tiny houses, cabins, nature lodges, caves, and more. As to be expected, glamping is more expensive than camping since you're provided with almost everything you need, except the clothes and footwear you would need for any excursions. You don't have to bring your own tent, sleeping bag, stove, pots and pans, or eating utensils. Glamping services vary as well, from tents and yurts where you cook for yourself to full-service hut resorts and nature lodges with all meals included and personal butlers.

If you're new to camping and would like to ease into it instead of going straight from zero to roughing it, or if you'd just like to get a bit closer to nature than a typical rental condominium or hotel room, glamping is the way to achieve that. If you just need a break from sleeping on the ground in a tent, glamping can be a welcome change. The only risk is that you might like it so much that you may never go back to "real" camping.

Popular Destinations

Glamping Hub. This booking platform provides glamping listings for destinations all over the world. Listings are organized both by destination and type of glamping (such as yurt, tent cabin, canvas tent, treehouse, etc.), so you can start your search by where you want to stay or by what type of structure you wish to stay in.

Log Village and Grist Mill Campground (Upstate New York). On the site of a grist mill built in 1810 and the former village of log homes that surrounded it, this property sits between the Adirondack Park and Vermont's Green Mountains. Four yurts sleep six to eleven people each, with grills and access to a campfire pit.

Camp Ribbonwood (Warner Springs, California). With a large timber-frame tent for two people,

located on a fenced-in private ranch between San Diego and Los Angeles and six miles from the nearest town, this is a dog-friendly site, with full kitchen, pizza oven, grill, and fireplace.

Agafay Desert Luxury Camp (Morocco). Offering private tents with king- and queen-size beds, personal butler service, three-course dinners, and no electricity (candle and lantern light only), this resort an hour from Marrakech is posh, but it gets you up close to the desert.

Tailwind Jungle Lodge (Nayarit, Mexico). This jungle retreat on the coast near Puerto Vallarta features a range of accommodations: thatched-roof palapas and casitas, plus safari tents for the more adventurous, all with full kitchens and private showers.

Gear

A glamping trip doesn't require any special gear. This is, of course, dependent on what's provided by the host of your destination, so make sure you know what you need before you go. Things that may or may not be provided could include daypacks (for hiking), flashlights, bedding (including extra blankets), toiletries, and/or firewood.

Above: Glamping resorts include private or communal restrooms and showers. **Right:** A couple shops at a country market for dinner supplies.

Top: A signed hiking trail leads into a forest. **Above:** Board games, word games, and card games are great ways to pass the time; most glamping resorts will have an assortment available for guests. **Left:** Another benefit of glamping: provided grills make for an exceptional dinner.

"LIGHT A CAMPFIRE AND
EVERYONE'S A STORYTELLER."

–JOHN J. GEDDES

Build a Campfire

Here's the most important thing when building a campfire: Make sure it won't get out of control. If you're at a campground, there should be an existing fire ring at your campsite. If not, build a ring about eight inches high out of rocks that are approximately fist-size in diameter, to keep the fire from getting away from you. Next, stack your fuel in a small pyramid, starting with dry tinder (small shards of leftover firewood, newspaper, dry bark, etc.), building a small tepee of kindling (pinky-diameter or smaller sticks or pieces of wood) above that, and on top of that, a larger pyramid of narrower pieces of firewood (wrist-diameter or so). Once you've got that constructed, take your lighter or matches and light the tinder in three or four places, watching the flames closely. As the tinder ignites, it should start to burn the kindling. Blow gently on the burning tinder to deliver oxygen to keep the fire climbing up to the kindling and then to the firewood; don't blow so hard the flame goes out. As the firewood begins to burn, keep an eye on it. Add more pieces of wood as the fire burns and collapses, making sure it's getting enough oxygen to keep going. Remember, you don't have to construct a huge fire—just something big enough to provide ambience and warmth.

KINDLING

FIREWOOD

DRY TINDER

School-Night Camping Feels Like Getting Away with Something

The scene: Eight friends gather in a city park in central Denver near a group of bicycles. The bikes are loaded down with tents, sleeping bags, and food. Some of the group members tote large backpacks. Two bikes have attached trailers, one with a half-dozen camp chairs strapped to it, the other a baby trailer with two bundles of firewood bought at a nearby convenience store. The sun is still high in the sky as the sound of rush-hour traffic gradually decreases. When the last of the group has arrived, everyone stands their bicycles up, gingerly mounts them, and starts pedaling toward the nearest paved bike path.

For the next seventy-five minutes, the group forms a motley peloton on the bike path, switching the order, riding in three or four pairs or in groups of three. Twice they stop to resecure loads to their bike frames. As the sun lowers into its final hour above the horizon, the group rolls into a state park campground and picks a campsite among the trees but within earshot of the low hum of car traffic from the freeway less than a mile away. The cyclists unpack their bikes, set up tents and camp chairs, and dump their food onto the picnic table. Someone takes initiative and lights a campfire, even though the temperature won't get colder than sixty-five degrees that evening.

Does that sound like a good Thursday night? It *was* a good Thursday night, in my memory. This is exactly what a group of friends and I used to do a couple times each summer—bike camping on a "school night." All of us had nine-to-five jobs, but we'd take one Thursday evening to get together at six o'clock, pedal a little more than an hour from the middle of the city out to the nearest public campground, and go camping. In the morning, we'd all get up at different times in order to make it into work on time (some of us could get away with not showering before work on Fridays; some of us had to look a little more presentable). It always felt like we were getting away with something, since almost everyone reserves camping for weekends or vacation days. Most people wouldn't bat an eye at a coworker who shows up to the office on a Friday after staying out a little late the previous night at a concert or a baseball game. But camping on a Thursday night? Not that common at my office, for sure. Sneaking in a weeknight camp is actually much more feasible than one might think, though. All it takes is a little planning and coordination with friends.

You may not get to settle into camping mode 100 percent on a school night. You'll probably have to skip the leisurely morning of drinking coffee in a camp chair for an hour or two, and it's more hectic trying to figure out your work commute from a campsite instead of your home. But even one quick night under the stars can be enough to provide relief from urban life. Plenty of us live a lot closer to nature than we think, and even if the nearby campgrounds are more suburban than middle of nowhere, it's still camping. And here's a secret: Most campgrounds aren't crowded on weeknights. All this adventure takes is a little initiative and planning to sneak in some extra camping nights during the summer. And maybe a few friends willing to try the same idea.

Everyone who has ever gone backpacking, from first-timers to folks on their nintieth straight day on the Appalachian Trail, has wondered the same thing: *Is my backpack too heavy?* Aficionados of ultralight backpacking would probably say the same thing to all of us: Yes, it is. And there's one way to fix it: Take fewer things with you on the trail.

Ultralight backpacking to a view along the Four Pass Loop, Colorado

Sounds simple, doesn't it? It is, until you look at your gear and have to decide what to bring and what to leave behind. Everything that makes you comfortable in the backcountry adds weight, and as the saying goes, "Ounces equal pounds, and pounds equal pain." Leaving something at home means you won't have it when you're camping, but it also means you won't have to deal with the weight of it on your back while you're hiking.

Extra pair of shoes for when you get to camp? Probably not worth the pounds. Extra shirts that don't smell like you've been hiking in them all day? Carry one spare; more will just add ounces to your pack. Camp pillow? Use a balled-up jacket or a stuff sack full of clothes instead. A bowl to eat out of and a mug to drink coffee from? Leave the bowl behind and use the same cup to eat breakfast and then drink coffee (or vice versa). Five-pound tent? Take only the rainfly and footprint and save yourself a couple pounds (but only if you're going somewhere without mosquitoes).

True ultralight backpacking experts will tell you that to really minimize your pack weight, you need to weigh all your gear with a scale, make a spreadsheet of all the gear you plan to take, then be ruthless about cutting items (and weight). This is a good tactic, but only to the extent that you are prepared to make sacrifices for lower pack weight.

Even if you're not trying to camp savagely ultralight, you can probably shave weight from your pack by being brutally honest with yourself: Can you stand wearing the same two shirts for a week? (Probably.) Can you survive without an extra pair of shoes for camp? (Quite likely.) Do you need two paperback books for a four-day trek? (How about one book, or an e-reader app on your phone that carries dozens of books without adding a gram of weight to your backpack?)

One of the easiest, but often more expensive, ways to cut weight is to replace old backpacking gear. Tents, backpacks, sleeping bags, and sleeping pads have gotten lighter in the past few years, and that trend will continue.

Almost all outdoor retailers provide information on the weight of all the gear they sell, so you can compare and decide what's worth spending money on and what isn't.

If you're eager to chop pack weight to the absolute minimum, you'll find no shortage of Internet forums, websites, and YouTube channels dedicated to different strategies and special (sometimes homemade) gear. One note of caution: Most people who push the envelope of minimalist backpacking have lots of experience and have honed their needs according to years of hiking. Because it's hard to know what you can live without on the trail without some experimentation, it's usually better to make your first backpacking forays with a little too much gear and trim down from there.

Even if you're not looking to savagely cut pounds and ounces until you're down to the absolute minimum of essentials to keep you alive in the elements, learning a little bit about ultralight backpacking principles and techniques can save you a solid chunk of weight in your backpack.

Gear

Alcohol stove. Ultralight backpackers are famous for fashioning simple stoves out of beer cans or cat food cans—there are no moving parts, and alcohol fuel is widely available. Several companies make alcohol stoves (not out of beer cans!) for purchase. Note that alcohol stoves aren't quite as easy to control as most backpacking stoves, so use caution when lighting them in fire-prone areas (such as the entire Mountain West in the summertime).

Ultralight backpack. Most backpacks for weeklong trips weigh four to five pounds, but ultralight packs can weigh as little as two pounds. Be warned that some of that weight is saved by eliminating comfort features like support stays and padding, so ultralight packs won't feel like big, comfy backpacks—but if you're packing light anyway, you might not notice.

Ultralight sleeping pads. Many ultralight backpackers cut weight by switching out cushy sleeping pads for three-quarter-length pads (which provide padding for head, shoulders, and hips but not lower legs) and using their backpack or clothes to pad their lower legs and feet. Other ultralight pad designs eliminate sections of cushioning and/or use lighter-weight materials to save ounces.

Tarp. Contemporary backpacking tents are lighter than ever, but a tarp is almost always a lighter option when backpacking—especially if you're already carrying trekking poles, which double as poles for rigging most backpacking tarps at the end of the day, when you're done hiking. So instead of carrying a tent, rainfly, and tent poles, carry a sub-one-pound tarp. A tarp may not be quite as effective at keeping out rain (and bugs and critters), though, so keep that in mind.

Top Left: A trail contours along an alpine slope. **Above:** A backpacker fills out a wilderness permit at a trailhead. **Left:** A trailhead map shows the immediate area's topography and trails.

Clean Out Your Tent

Your tent, like you, will get dirty while camping. Be cautious with food and beverages inside your tent, because bears and critters like food, and they may decide to investigate or inhabit your tent at some point in your trek if good smells waft out of it. So the first step in maintaining your tent is to keep it as clean as possible during the trip. You'll get rocks, dirt, and other natural solids inside the tent, but should you spill food, drink, or scented products, clean those promptly and thoroughly.

Unless things get completely out of control during your trip, wait to clean your tent until you're packing up to leave. Once your sleeping bags and gear are out of the tent, remove the stakes, unzip the door (or doors), pick the tent up by the poles, lift it over your head, and shake it, letting the dirt and rocks fall to the ground. That should get most of the dirt out of the tent.

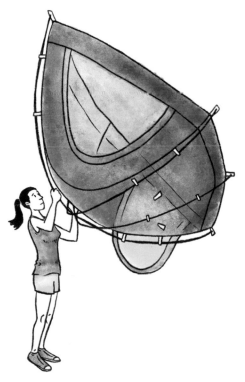

When you arrive home, set up the tent in your garage, living room, yard, or nearby park and let it dry. Even without rain, condensation can build up on the tent, and that will turn into mold if you just pack the tent and fly away and forget about them. If something doesn't brush or shake out, wipe it down with a wet rag or paper towel. Plain water should do the trick, but if it doesn't, use a product that's designed for tent fabrics, or clean with plain soapy water. Avoid household cleaning products, because some can damage tent fabrics. Let the tent fabric dry completely before you pack it up again.

Popular
Destinations

All backpacking destinations are popular
for ultralight backpacking, but you'll see
more ultralight practitioners on longer
trails, specifically the Pacific Crest Trail, the
Continental Divide Trail, and the Appalachian
Trail. Walking for a couple thousand miles makes
people very conscious of the weight in their
packs, and most PCT, CDT, and AT thru-hikers
are extremely minimal in what they carry. Long-
distance trails aren't just an American thing,
either—Jordan's 400-mile Jordan Trail, New
Zealand's 1,864-mile Te Araroa trek, and Chile's
1,700-mile Route of Parks trail have all opened
in the past decade.

Left: Rocks hold down the corners of a tent at a sandy campsite where stakes won't work. **Below:** An ultralight backpacking camp setup includes a simple tarp, sleeping bag, and sleeping pad. **Bottom Left**: A bear canister sits ready to be locked tight for the evening.

Top left: A backpacker uses a luggage scale to weigh their pack at the trailhead. **Above:** Gaiters are useful for keeping rocks and sand out of hiking shoes.

Camping Solo

If leaving our hectic lives to get into nature is an act of rebellion in our society of busyness, heading out alone is an act of revolution. Time spent alone at a campground or in the backcountry, watching a fire or just sitting and listening to the sounds of a forest, can be a revelation. The silence may be uncomfortable at first, and we may feel like something is missing, but once we've experienced the mental reset solitude provides, silence can be compelling, too.

Yes, friends are fun when camping—but they aren't mandatory. Whether you've never been camping or just never camped by yourself, pay attention on the trail: You'll be surprised by how many people are doing it alone.

Most of us hesitate before going out to dinner or a movie by ourselves, let alone backpacking or camping. But you can find a setup and comfort level that works for you. Some of us feel safer in a campground full of other people. Others of us feel safer ten miles from the nearest road, where we won't see another (human) soul for days.

Writer and photographer Emily Pennington has made a career out of traveling alone in the backcountry. On her first solo backpacking trip, she picked a trail she had hiked before, one where she knew she'd see plenty of other backpackers—and she was still scared. But only for a little while.

"I soon learned that there's nothing much to worry about, other than spraining your ankle or some other human error," she said. Since then, she's done nearly twenty solo camping and backpacking trips. She has two rules: Don't die, and don't do anything stupid—which means staying on trail just in case rescuers need to find her, and not taking unnecessary risks on steep, rocky terrain unless she has a climbing partner. Over the years, she hasn't found much cause to worry about other people in the outdoors.

"It might seem counterintuitive, but the strangers I've met on the trail (and even car camping) when I'm solo have been nothing but incredibly kind and eager to help," she said. "It can be easy to worry about unknowns when you're far away from civilization and no one can hear you scream, but for some reason, I think it is our shared humanity that gets brought out in wild spaces, rather than our demons. Hikers have given me food, offered me extra fuel, and let me borrow their ukulele in the backcountry. Just like in the city, there will be exceptions to the rule and bad actors, but the fact that you're all out there, roughing it together, seems to bring out the best in people."

Whatever your experience level, the most important thing to do when traveling solo is to tell someone where you're going, when to expect you back, and what to do and whom to call if you're not back by a certain date and time. For example: "I'm going backpacking starting Friday on the _____ trail in the _____ forest, and I plan on being back to my car by 1:00 p.m. on Sunday. If you don't hear from me by 7:00 p.m. on Sunday, please call the _____ county sheriff at 000-000-0000." *If something does happen, even just a sprained ankle, you'd much rather wait a few hours for a rescue than wait a few days.* Once you're prepared and your family or friends are informed, you can focus on enjoying the solitude (and the views).

An elaborate stairwell leads to a secluded treehouse in the forest in the Red River Gorge, Kentucky.

Perhaps you have a memory of your own or a friend's childhood treehouse: a single room, not too high off the ground, reached by a rope ladder or set of planks nailed to a tree trunk, maybe with a No Boys Allowed or No Girls Allowed sign to keep someone's brother or sister out. It was your little refuge among the leaves, even if it had no door or roof.

In the years since your childhood tree fort, treehouses have upped their game and become hideaways and vaction hotspots, using rope bridges, spiral staircases, floating supports, and other architectural and structural tricks to place aesthetic suites high in forest canopies. Think more "romantic getaway," less "clubhouse," with no limits on the possibilities besides the height of the trees they're built in.

Of course, there are a few concessions, because most treehouse stays are essentially a form of camping. Most treehouses don't have flush toilets, or the nearest one might be located a few steps from your bedroom—or more like a short walk and climb down a few ladders or staircases. Maybe you'll have running water, but more likely you'll have a small sink and a five-gallon tank of water. Don't expect room service. But that's not why you're here.

You're living in a tree for a night or two, which is a pretty fantastical situation to find yourself in. If the breeze blows the tree you're perched in, the building may sway a little. You'll be close to the birds, who might nest by your bedroom window. You are surrounded by great views, possibly without even having to hike up a mountain. And although you won't have concierge service, you also won't have neighbors next door or on the floor above, stomping on your ceiling.

Only a few dozen treehouse accommodations exist in the United States, so it's a unique niche. If you're willing to search them out, however, you're in for a memorable night or two.

Popular Destinations

Canopy Crew (Red River Gorge, Kentucky). Three different treehouses, including the Observatory, a two-building unit with a glass-ceilinged bedroom reached by two-hundred-plus stairs.

TreeHouse Point (Issaquah, Washington). Six different treehouses located a thirty-minute drive from downtown Seattle.

Treehouse Cottages (Eureka Springs, Arkansas). Three different treehouses perched twenty-plus feet off the ground, but only a few minutes' walk from historic downtown Eureka Springs.

Free Spirit Spheres (Vancouver Island, British Columbia). Literal spheres suspended or perched in trees, each with sleeping accommodations for two or three people, plus full private bathrooms a short walk away.

Mind, Body, and Spirit (Atlanta, Georgia). Airbnb's most coveted listing in the world: a trio of treehouses, each serving as a different room, connected by rope bridges.

Gear

Most treehouse stays are closer to glamping than camping: They have beds, linens, sometimes a water supply, and some sort of composting toilet. Depending on the amenities offered in your particular treehouse, you may want to bring:
• Sleeping bag
• Warm layers
• Rain jacket
• Headlamp
• Coffee-making device or instant coffee
• Firewood

"WHEN ONE TUGS AT A SINGLE THING
IN NATURE, HE FINDS IT ATTACHED TO
THE REST OF THE WORLD."

—JOHN MUIR, *THE YOSEMITE*

Right: A door leads to the composting toilet adjacent to a treehouse. **Far Right:** Guests use a caged ladder to climb from the kitchen to the bedroom. **Bottom Right:** All spaces in a small treehouse are used efficiently, right down to hanging mugs next to the sink. **Below:** The treehouse has multilevel sleeping quarters.

Above: A mesh hammock built into the treehouse deck is the perfect spot for reading. **Right:** A good selection of books helps pass a rainy afternoon.

Stay Warm in a Sleeping Bag

Sleeping bags are simple, wonderful inventions that use human body heat to keep us warm in even subzero temperatures. That said, they work better if you use them properly, by following a few simple rules.

First, buy the correct sleeping bag for your outings. Read the temperature ratings conservatively—a forty-five-degree bag will probably keep you alive at forty-five degrees Fahrenheit, but not comfortable. If it gets colder than the bag's rating, you'll likely be miserable.

Second, if it's cold outside, wearing more clothes inside your sleeping bag won't necessarily keep you warmer (the bag needs to reflect your body heat back to you). But wearing the right clothes will make a difference. Before you climb into your sleeping bag for the night, change out of wet/damp clothes, including socks. Wearing a down jacket inside your sleeping bag and a beanie can add warmth as well.

Third, zip up your bag so only your face is poking out. Don't put your mouth inside the bag—your breath will condense into moisture on the inside of the bag, and you'll get cold. Cinch the bag around your face so drafts can't creep in, then get comfy. When you roll onto your side in the night, make sure your sleeping bag rotates with you, so your mouth and nose still stick out.

Finally, if you are too warm in the night, don't unzip the whole sleeping bag—try venting it in increments. Unzip it a little, maybe pull your head farther out of the bag. If that doesn't work, slide the zipper down a few inches or a foot. Keep adjusting as the night goes on.

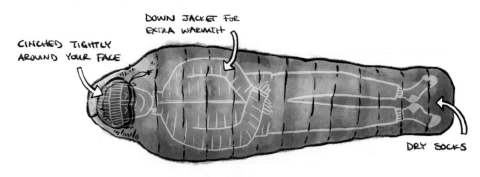

We often refer to camping as "sleeping under the stars." Lots of times, however, we end up sleeping with something between us and the heavens—a tent's rainfly or the roof of a van or car—to protect us from things like rain and mosquitoes and no-see-ums.

But with the right weather forecast, truly sleeping under the stars, or "bivying," can be a wonderful experience. You sleep in fresh air, as opposed to the clammy air and humid condensation inside a tent. When you look up, you see a blanket of stars. There's no need to set up a tent—or take it down the next morning. You don't have to unzip multiple zippers if you need to get up in the middle of the night. And of course, you don't have to locate a perfectly flat six- by four-foot spot to stake down a tent—you simply find a spot big enough for your sleeping bag, which opens up all kinds of possibilities for great morning views.

If you don't have a 100 percent clear-weather forecast, you can hang a tarp and still get a fresh-air, zipper-free night—one with modest protection from the elements. It's all about how close to nature you want to be (or how badly you don't want to deal with a tent). Another option is a bivy sack, a waterproof cover that slides onto a sleeping bag and provides weather protection overnight. If it starts to rain hard in the night, you might pull your backpack or other gear inside your bivy sack to keep it dry. If you're bivying and want to protect your sleeping bag from punctures, place a light tarp or tent footprint under your sleeping pad to keep sharp objects from poking through.

You might be concerned about snakes, mice, or other critters sneaking into your sleeping bag in the night, and that's a reasonable worry. But it's unlikely a snake will try to enter your sleeping bag while you're in it—the sleeping bag's job is to reflect your body heat inward, not project it outward, where a cold snake would search it out for warmth. To be completely safe if you get up in the middle of the night to use the bathroom, just check your sleeping bag or shake it out when you return—you'd be more likely (but still quite unlikely) to find a scorpion in there than a snake. Probably the biggest concern is ticks. If you're in an area known for ticks, give serious thought as to whether you want to bivy.

Another possible side effect of camping without a tent is condensation forming on your sleeping bag during the night—a large amount can soak a down-filled sleeping bag and, depending on how wet it gets, reduce the bag's insulation value to almost nothing. If you camp next to a lake or river or in a very humid environment, take condensation into consideration before forgoing a tent for the night.

Gear

Bivy sack. A waterproof cover for a sleeping bag, a bivy sack will keep you dry in inclement weather and provide a good amount of insulation from wind and a small amount of insulation from cold.

Tarp. A tarp can provide similar weather protection to a tent, but with much more airflow, and if you're backpacking, a backpacking-specific tarp will be much lighter than almost any tent.

If you're not expecting rain, the tarp can be used under your sleeping pad to protect it from sharp sticks or other objects that might puncture the pad.

Mosquito net. If you're camping in mosquito habitat and don't want to take a tent, a small head net can keep your face protected (which should be the only part of your body exposed when you zip up your sleeping bag).

Popular
Destinations

Pretty much any camping destination is good for
tentless camping, with the caveats of good weather,
no ticks, and no biting insects. Certain environments,
like the more arid Mountain West and the Southwest
desert or Jordan's desert valleys, are particularly
good for sleeping without a tent. Some boaters on
Grand Canyon raft trips are able to go their entire trip
without using a tent at all.

Opposite Page; Top Left: When camping without a tent, gear sits directly on the ground. **Top Right:** A light backpacking stove is set up just outside the tarp. **Bottom Left:** A lightweight tent stake holds the corner of a tarp in place in rocky ground. **Bottom Right:** Rain beads up on the outside of a waterproof bivy sack, but the camper doesn't get wet.

Above: The unobstructed views are remarkable when you're camping without a tent; here the sunset peeks out underneath a building storm above a desert canyon.

Set Up a Tarp

Tents are great, but no tent is truly as minimalist as a classic tarp. To set one up, you need only two trees at least fifteen feet apart, about fifty feet of lightweight cord, eight tent stakes, and a tarp that's roughly ten by ten feet (or eight by six feet, twelve by ten feet, etc.). Once you've found your two trees, tie your cord around the trees so it's taut in the middle and about four feet above the ground. Set the tarp on top of the cord so the tarp is bisected, and tie short sections of cord to each corner grommet. To form a classic A-frame, pull the four attached cords away from the center of the tarp so that each cord is taut and the corners of the tent are suspended above the ground. Attach small pieces of cord to each remaining grommet and do the same with those to fully secure all sides of the tarp. Consider a couple things: Since there are no mesh windows or doors on a tarp, you're sharing your space with whatever insects may be around. Also, any precipitation besides gentle, perfectly vertically falling rain is likely to make its way through the ends of your tarp, so sleep a good distance from each end to avoid waking up with a wet sleeping bag.

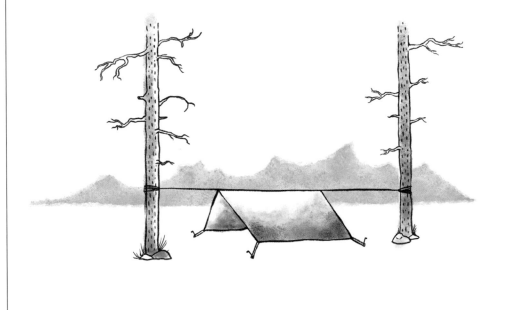

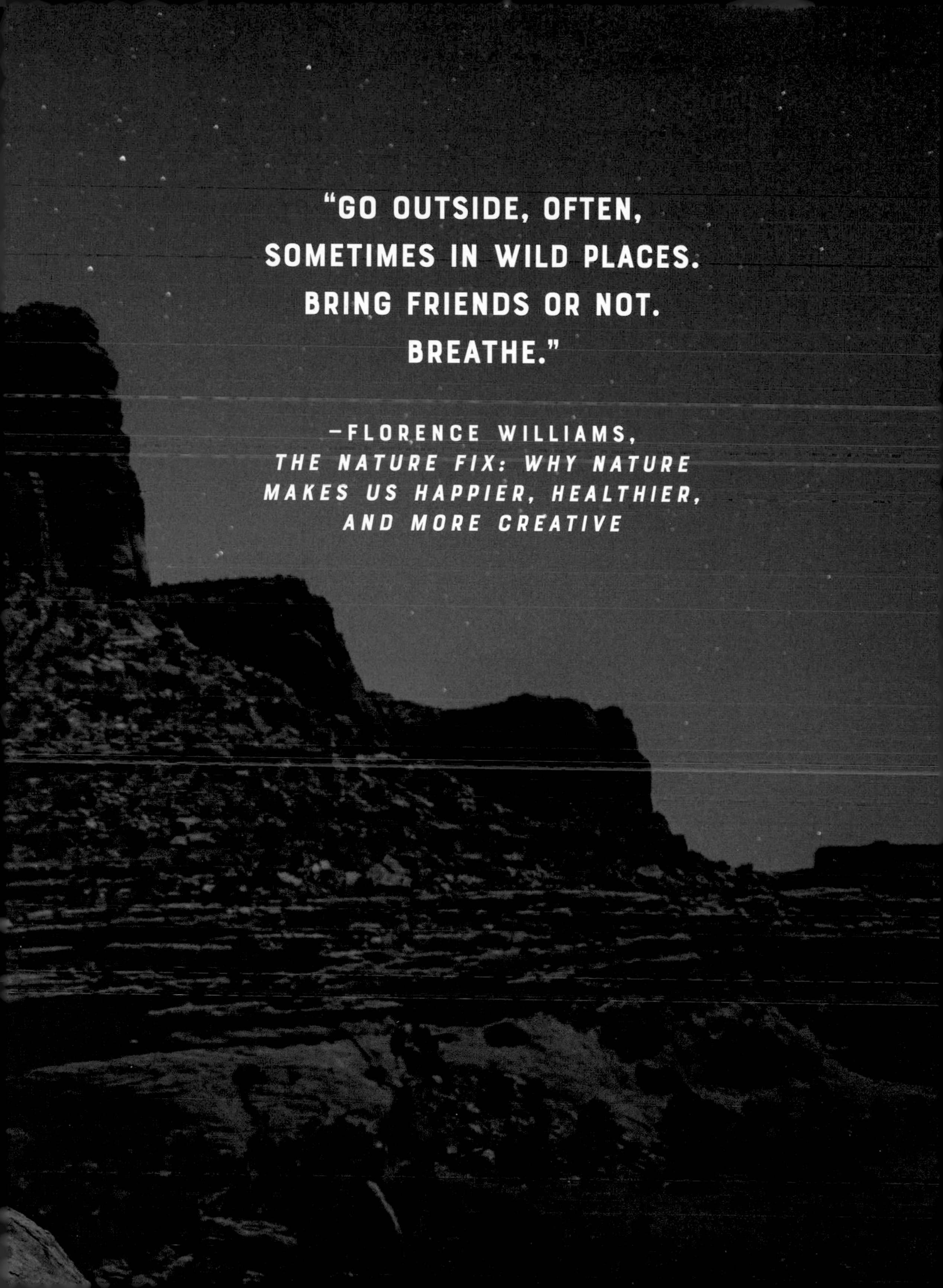

"GO OUTSIDE, OFTEN,
SOMETIMES IN WILD PLACES.
BRING FRIENDS OR NOT.
BREATHE."

—FLORENCE WILLIAMS,
*THE NATURE FIX: WHY NATURE
MAKES US HAPPIER, HEALTHIER,
AND MORE CREATIVE*

Epilogue: Leaving It Better Than You Found It

Why do we love mountains and deserts and rivers? One reason: They're still wild. For the most part, they haven't been altered in thousands of years. They've been spared from the overtaking of land for parking lots and big-box stores. They're different from the places we live and work, in that they're largely unaffected by humans. Sure, there are trails, and roads to those trails, and other infrastructure that enables us to reach our favorite vistas, but no more than is necessary.

We love camping for the same reasons: A campsite may offer a spot big enough for a tent, maybe a fire ring, and sometimes a picnic table, but it still feels wild. Our favorite campsites are the ones that feel like they are our own, like no one's been there for a while and we have the spot to ourselves. They're gifts we receive from past users and can pay forward to the next visitors with minimal effort. All we have to do is not wreck the place, put our fires out, not cut tree branches down, and take our trash with us when we leave. It's that simple.

Now what if you want to leave your wild area *better* than you found it? That also is not difficult—and it's exponentially better for the land and for your fellow outdoorsmen and -women. Pick up one or two extra pieces of trash and pack them with your stuff. Don't build a new fire ring if one exists nearby. Don't plop your tent down on live vegetation if a tent space has obviously been established. And don't leave behind objects that weren't there when you arrived—with one exception: If you're car camping and you have extra firewood on your last day, leave it for the next person.

If we leave a wild place just 1 percent better than it was when we found it, and everyone following us does the same, then the places where we made our best memories will be places our children and grandchildren can make memories, too.

Resources

Planning and How-To

Adventure Cycling Association—Guided tours, routes, maps, planning, and bicycle touring information
adventurecycling.org

Backpacking Light—Tips, how-tos, and gear reviews for ultralight backpacking and hiking
backpackinglight.com

Bikepacking.com—Bikepacking how-tos and routes all over the world
bikepacking.com

Gaia GPS—USGS topo maps for downloading to your phone for use offline
https://www.gaiagps.com/

Glamping Hub—Find and book glamping accommodations anywhere
glampinghub.com

Hiking Project—Hiking trails around the United States and the world; save maps and info to your phone
hikingproject.com

HipCamp—Find and book campsites on private land
hipcamp.com

Leave No Trace—Principles for minimizing your environmental footprint
lnt.org

Retailers

Backcountry
https://www.backcountry.com/

Bass Pro Shops
https://www.basspro.com/

Cabela's
https://www.cabelas.com/

Campmor
https://www.campmor.com/

Dick's Sporting Goods
https://www.dickssportinggoods.com/

Eastern Mountain Sports
https://www.ems.com/

L.L. Bean
www.llbean.com

Moosejaw
https://www.moosejaw.com/

Mountain Equipment Co-operative
https://www.mec.ca/en/

REI
www.rei.com

Acknowledgments

Thanks to Judy Pray and the team at Artisan Books, who made this book a reality but didn't get to see nearly as many sunsets, sunrises, and campfires as we did (on a positive note, they didn't have to smell us after four days of backpacking, either).

To our friends who joined us on these trips and let Forest take dozens of photos of them: Thank you. You know who you are: Amy O'Connell, Hilary Oliver, Ashlee Langholz, Laura Yale, Ani Yahzid, Casey Allee-Jumbo, Stefan Hunt, Vanessa Marian, Canyon Woodward, Will Handsfield, Brett Poirier, Graham Zimmerman, Brody Leven, Steve Casimiro, Chris El-Deiry, Natalie El-Deiry, Julian El-Deiry, Abi FitzGerald, Mitsu Iwasaki, Max Lowe, Isaac Lowe-Anker, Charles Post, and Rachel Pohl.

To Carl Johnson and Big Agnes, and to Vince Mazzuca and Osprey: Thanks for helping us out with fantastic tents and backpacks to make these backcountry missions not only possible but comfortable.

Thanks to Django Kroner and the Canopy Crew for accommodating us in treehouses in the Red River Gorge, and thanks to David Troya, Jessica Armstrong, and Amy Ahlblad at Glamping Hub and Hilary Oreschnick at the Log Village and Grist Mill Campground for hosting us as glamping guests.

Forest would like to thank: Mom and Dad for making camping such a big part of our growing-up years, and Laura Yale for backpacking through a lightning storm on our first date.

Brendan would like to thank: Hilary Oliver for putting up with some of these shenanigans, participating in others, and tolerating me being away from home dozens of days and nights to make a book about camping.

Index

About the Authors

Writer **Brendan Leonard** and photographer
Forest Woodward have been adventuring together
since 2012, when they met on a climb of Mount
Whitney in Sequoia National Park in California.
They have skied off summits, shared ropes, run
hundreds of miles of trails, lived off rafts and
kayaks, drunk dozens of gallons of coffee, gotten
cold, wet, exhausted, chafed, bitten, scratched, and
stormed on, but mostly had fun together, and have
collaborated on several award-winning short films.
This is their first book together.

Library of Congress Cataloging-in-Publication Data

Names: Leonard, Brendan, author. | Woodward, Forest, author.
Title: The camping life / Brendan Leonard and Forest Woodward.
Description: New York : Artisan, a division of Workman Publishing Co.,
    Inc., 2020. | Includes index.
Identifiers: LCCN 2019051154 | ISBN 9781579658434 (hardcover)
Subjects: LCSH: Camping—Handbooks, manuals, etc. | Backpacking—
Handbooks, manuals, etc. | Outdoor recreation—Handbooks, manuals, etc.
Classification: LCC GV191.7 .L46 2020 | DDC 796.54—dc23
LC record available at https://lccn.loc.gov/2019051154

Design by Heitman-Ford + Co.

Artisan books are available at special discounts when purchased in
bulk for premiums and sales promotions as well as for fund-raising or
educational use. Special editions or book excerpts also can be created
to specification. For details, contact the Special Sales Director at the
address below, or send an e-mail to specialmarkets@workman.com.

For speaking engagements, contact speakersbureau@workman.com.

Published by Artisan
A division of Workman Publishing Co., Inc.
225 Varick Street
New York, NY 10014-4381
artisanbooks.com

Artisan is a registered trademark of Workman Publishing Co., Inc.

Published simultaneously in Canada by Thomas Allen & Son, Limited

Printed in China

First printing, March 2020

10 9 8 7 6 5 4 3 2 1